Dismantling American Common Law

Dismantling American Common Law

Liberty and Justice in Our Transformed Courts

Kyle Scott

LEXINGTON BOOKS
A division of
ROWMAN & LITTLEFIELD PUBLISHERS, INC.
Lanham • Boulder • New York • Toronto • Plymouth, UK

LEXINGTON BOOKS

A division of Rowman & Littlefield Publishers, Inc.
A wholly owned subsidiary of The Rowman & Littlefield Publishing Group, Inc.
4501 Forbes Boulevard, Suite 200
Lanham, MD 20706

Estover Road
Plymouth PL6 7PY
United Kingdom

British Library Cataloguing in Publication Information Available

Library of Congress Cataloging-in-Publication Data

Scott, Kyle, 1977–
Dismantling American common law : liberty and justice in our transformed courts / Kyle Scott.
p. cm.
Includes bibliographical references and index.
ISBN-13: 978-0-7391-2376-8 (cloth : alk. paper)
ISBN-10: 0-7391-2376-9 (pbk. : alk. paper)
1. Common law—United States. 2. Jury—United States. 3. Judicial process—United States. I. Title.
KF394.S395 2007
340.5'70973—dc22 2007036693

Printed in the United States of America

∞™ The paper used in this publication meets the minimum requirements of American National Standard for Information Sciences—Permanence of Paper for Printed Library Materials, ANSI/NISO Z39.48–1992.

Contents

Acknowledgments

I have received support and encouragement from many sources, but let me begin by thanking my family. Without the help of my entire family, each giving aid in their own way, I might have given up long ago. To my father, without whom this project and my graduate career would not have been possible, I give special thanks. While he may not have always understood or approved of what I was doing, he never stopped supporting me and giving me the encouragement I needed. This speaks highly of his character as a man and his quality as a father. My mother and sister are also deserving of special thanks, as they provided words of advice and a shoulder to lean on when times were tough. These two women possess a strength that I can only hope to duplicate. Equally important was the support of my wife, whose encouragement gave me the ability to continue where I might not have otherwise been able to, and whose presence in my life gives this project and all others meaning. The amount of selflessness and patience my wife displayed while I went through this process shows just how much more I can learn from her than she can from me. To my son Braden, who makes leaving for work nearly impossible and makes returning home the best part of my day, thank you for letting Daddy work.

I would also like to thank Paul Brace for aiding me in the dissertation that this book is a revision of. His commitment to political science and encyclopedic knowledge of the discipline is unmatched, and should serve as a model for all graduate students. The insightful comments from Donald Lutz and James Kirby Martin at the dissertation stage were greatly appreciated.

I would like to thank my teacher, the late Ross Lence. My father once told me that if a son wants to show his parents how much he appreciates them, then he must become a good father himself. So it is, I believe, equally true with teachers. The debt I owe to Professor Lence can never be repaid, and his importance cannot be given justice by the words within my grasp, but I wish to show my gratitude by fulfilling my potential as a teacher and scholar. Unfortunately he has left this earth. His death has left a void in me that I will hopelessly try to fill with great books and eager students.

I would like to thank the Earhart Foundation for providing financial support during the year it took to complete the dissertation and Miami University (Ohio) where I worked on the revisions during the two years it took to bring this project to print.

For all those who helped on this project and who have been acknowledged, you are off the hook. All of the errors still present within this project are the burden of the author alone.

Introduction

The American system of law has experienced a quiet revolution that has gone largely unnoticed by political scientists and legal scholars. The change that has occurred—the dismantling of the American common law—has important consequences for democratic politics and our judicial system. The importance of studying the American common law does not end at American shores. This book addresses a fundamentally important topic in American law and politics with implications for broader questions about liberal democracy and constitutionalism in an era in which the movement around the world is toward democratic expansion and consolidation of new liberal democracies.

The American founding has received more than its fair share of scholarly attention. Authors ranging from Jack Rakove, to Gordon S. Wood, to Bernard Bailyn, to Charles Beard have contributed to our knowledge of this period. Efforts have been made to settle disputes over what philosophers were most influential on the thought of the founders, what the goal of the founders was in establishing a new government, and what political philosophy can be drawn out of the American founding. One of the most recognized efforts is that undertaken by Forrest McDonald. In 1985 he published his influential, if controversial, *Novus Ordo Seclorum: The Intellectual Origins of the Constitution*. McDonald's analysis does not attribute American political philosophy at the time of the founding to any single school but says Americans assimilated a number of European thinkers to create their own brand of liberal government. But even among the founders were disparate views of what government should be and ought to do. The divergent views of the founders are attributed to the diverse sources from which they drew. But McDonald does give great weight to the impact of the Scottish Enlightenment. While these studies are interesting and deserve the attention they receive, this book feels they stop short of addressing other pressing matters; most specifically, understanding the influence the founding has had on modern politics. Scholars such as McDonald do little to tell us why what they study is important to the modern reader.

This study sets out to demonstrate that the parameters which confine modern politics were set in place at the time of the founding. The path which the American regime has followed was the path set forth by the founders. In order to address these topics one can trace the development of the American common law, and subsequent dismantling, to show that the creation of a judiciary controlled system, that consolidates political power at the national level, is a result of the thought of Alexander Hamilton as influenced by William Blackstone and Charles de Secondat, Baron de Montesquieu.

The common law is characterized by its use of juries, precedent, a distinction between courts of law and equity, a strict reliance on procedure, and uncodified law. The common law was established to guarantee fair trials and governance by the rule of law with respect to local interests. The common law recognizes the need to respect tradition and custom, which is why it can only be practiced at the level closest to the people. This formulation is consistent with what James Stoner says is part of the essence of common law. "Common law emphasizes assent rather than domination, the community rather than the state, moral authority rather than physical power" (Stoner 2003, 8).

The common law is not rigid; it is adaptable, just as the community that it is derived from has changing needs and considerations. Thus, codification is contrary to common law. While revision of statutes is possible, codification violates the essence of common law. Furthermore, common law decisions reflect the sentiment of the community; common law must be made locally in order to reflect this sentiment as the national stage is too far removed from the people to be truly responsive. Judges must be able, with the aid of the jury, to hand down decisions which best serve the interests of the community. While not all laws are defined under this system, traditionally those laws left undefined by the legislature are left for the courts and the community to define through tradition, practice, and history. More to the point, the common law is not positive law. It relies on the belief that a moral sense of right and wrong is possessed by each individual in a community. It has a natural right foundation. This conceptualization of law is quite different from the statutory outlook. Common law understands that the role of law is to be representative of the people, held accountable by the people, and willed by the people in such a way that promotes the common good.

Though the judge is tempered by the jury, the judge is not confined by the jury. In addition to the populist strand of the common law described above, the common law is also found in fundamental documents which serve as repositories of common law jurisprudence. These documents contain natural rights which judges, as experts, are empowered to interpret and apply. The judicial perpetuation of natural rights in the common law setting can be seen by looking at the development of due process rights. The due process rights embodied in the U.S. Constitution and its Amendments can be traced back to the Magna Carta. The first version of the document was signed in 1215 by John, King of England and Ireland. In 1225 King Henry III executed chapter 29 of the Magna Carta, which was an extension and confirmation of chapter 39 in the first version. Both sections embody what Americans now recognize as procedural due process rights.

Beginning in 1205 King John and Pope Innocent III embarked on a struggle that led to King John's excommunication in 1209. In order to have the excommunication withdrawn, King John turned over England and Ireland to the papacy in 1213. King John's actions led to a revolt by the English barons for his violation of feudal law and custom. On June 15, 1215, in order to end the conflict between the barons and himself, King John signed the Magna Carta.

At the heart of the Great Charter were due process protections that would prevent the King from imposing new rules and penalties without first adhering to a fair and proper process. In chapter 52, King John agreed that anyone who "has been dispossessed or removed by us, without the legal judgment of his peers, from his lands, castles, or from his right, we will immediately restore them to him." Chapter 55 said that "fines, made with us unjustly and against the law of the land, . . . shall be entirely remitted." Chapters 20–22 provided equivalent protection for merchants, freemen, clergy, and barons. Chapter 39 was the boldest statement of due process. The chapter reads

> No freeman shall be arrested, or detained in prison, or deprived of his freehold, or in any way molested; and the King will not set forth against him, nor send against him, unless by the lawful judgment of his peers or by the law of the land. (Magna Carta, 1215)

This chapter protected all freemen from improper deprivation of their lives, liberties, or properties without due process under existing and proper laws. Historian Arthur Hogue comments that "The common law of the twelfth and thirteenth centuries is in large part the law of land and tenures, the law of property rights and services together with rules of procedure for the administration of justice" (Hogue 1986, 112).

The original charter was short-lived, however. On August 24, 1215, Pope Innocent III repealed the charter at the urging of King John. But, even the repeal did not last long as King Henry took over the throne in October 1216 after the death of King John. When the charter was reissued in 1225 it contained thirty-eight chapters and was proclaimed to be a reissue of the original charter. Although the commitment to the original charter was clear, chapter 29 of the new charter expanded and clarified chapter 39 of the original. In the new charter chapter 29 reads

> No freeman shall be taken, or imprisoned, or be disseised of his freehold, or liberties, or free customs, or be outlawed, or exiled, or any otherwise destroyed; nor will we not pass upon him, nor condemn him, but by lawful judgment of his peers, or by the law of the land. We will sell to no man, we will not deny or defer to any man either justice or right. (Magna Carta 1225)

The precise meaning of the Magna Carta would be determined by common law judges, the most famous of which was Edward Coke.

Lord Coke dedicated the Second Institute of his four-volume commentary *Institutes of the Laws of England* to the Magna Carta of 1225. Coke was as respected in America as he was in England. Coke writes, "by due process of the common law no man shall be put to answer without presentment before justices, or thing of record, or by due process, or by writ original" (Coke 1979, 50). Coke found the origins of the common law in the Magna Carta. Consequently he viewed the common law as a restraint on the powers of the monarchy and other governmental bodies. Coke understood due process to be found at common law when he writes that no man should be deprived of liberty or possessions, "without being brought in to answer but by due process of the common law" (Coke 1974, 50). Coke goes on to write that "the law of the land might extend to all, it is said *per legem terra* [by the law of the land]" (Coke 1974, 50).

The colonists brought with them the common law of England and made required reading out of Coke for most colonial lawyers. According to Edward Corwin, in the colonies Coke "was first on the ground" (Corwin 1928, 394). Coke was the embodiment of the common law. His authority was so strong that later commentators have written "that it is useless to contend that 'he was either misled by his sources or unconsciously misinterpreted them,' for Coke's mistakes, it is said, are the common law" (Brockelbank 1954, 562). Bernard Siegan writes, "English and American courts accepted and cited Coke's interpretation of chapter 29 as authoritative on the meaning of the 'law of the land' and the 'due process of law,' and numerous U.S. federal and state judicial opinions have cited him in various matters" (Siegan 2001, 12–13).

While Henry's charter provided provisions, there was no body instituted to provide for the protections. Coke reasoned, as others had, that it would be the role of English judges. "The judges had applied the common law to limit the king's powers as well as those of localities and guilds" (Siegan 2001, 15).

Coke told the Parliament in 1628 that "Magna Carta is such a fellow that he will have no Sovereign" (Gough 1971, 64 as quoted by Siegan 2001, 15). This proclamation is the very idea adopted by the American founding fathers, who designed a government to be one of laws and not of men. Coke derived his position from his own analysis of the Magna Carta and from the common law judges. Coke's position is most famously displayed in *Dr. Bonham's Case*. Thomas Bonham brought action for wrongful imprisonment against the president and censors of the College of Physicians in London. Coke presided over the case as the Chief Justice of the Court of Common Pleas. The decision of the court was for the plaintiff on the grounds that the statute violated common law principles. The case demonstrates the commitment on behalf of Coke to common law principles. Judges were placed in a new position as a result of the decision—a position in which they could decide on common law grounds even in cases where the parliament had spoken.

This line of thinking did not end with Coke. According to Chancellor James Kent:

> in republics it [the judiciary] is equally salutary, in protecting the constitution and laws from encroachment. . . . It is requisite that the courts of justice should be able, at all times, to present a determined countenance against all licentious acts; and to give them the firmness to do it. . . . (Kent 1836, 294)

Chancellor Kent made this quote in reference to individual due process rights and the ability, and responsibility, of a common law court to protect those rights. While Blackstone's assessment of the judiciary will not be explored until the final chapter of this book, it is appropriate to note at this point that in reference to the common law he wrote:

> Pursuant of the Magna Carta and by a variety of ancient statutes it is enacted that no man's lands or goods shall be seized into the king's hands, against the great charter, and the law of the land; and that no man shall be disinherited, nor put on of his franchises or freehold, unless he be duly brought to answer, and be forejudged by course of law; and if any thing be done to the contrary, it shall be redressed and holden for none. (Blackstone 1979, vol. I, 134–35)

These common law protections were imported to America. On September 5, 1774, the First Continental Congress declared that the rights of inhabitants of America are secured "by the immutable laws of nature, the principles of the English Constitution, and the several charters or compacts pursuant to which the colonial governments were established . . . the respective colonies are entitled to the common law of England" (Tansill 1972, 1–5). Even later Chancellor Kent recognized "It was not to be doubted that the constitution and laws of the United States were made in reference to the existence of the common law . . . the existence of the common law is not only supposed by the constitution, but it is appealed to for the construction of the interpretation of its powers" (Kent 1836, 315–16). Between 1776 and 1792 all thirteen of the former colonies put provisions into their state constitutions that mirrored those found in chapter 29 of the 1225 Magna Carta. Even the Northwest Ordinance provided a commitment to due process by saying, "no man shall be deprived of his life, liberty, or property, but by the judgment of his peers or the law of the land" (Tansill 1972, 48).

In these documents an articulation of natural rights is found. Thus the common law is more than simply the community's spirit. Judges who rise to the bench from the bar are well versed in these documents and should therefore help guide juries while not overriding the authority of juries. As will be shown throughout this book, the populist strand has been overwhelmed by this second strand resulting in a judiciary which is less attached to the common law principles that restrained judicial law making. Remember, principles of natural rights found in fundamental documents are not antithetical to populism. The way the common law has been dismantled has led to an abandonment of natural right doctrine that has been supplanted with a doctrine of government will. This has resulted in a violation of the populist strand of common law as well.

This study sets out to revisit the current American understanding of common law in order to understand what it was originally. Fortunately I am not alone in this effort, as others before me have shown the deleterious effects of abandoning the common law.

The slow and gradual deterioration of the common law has hampered its study since recognizing incremental change is sometimes difficult. This study provides a historical explanation supported by quantitative analysis to explain what factors have led to the dismantling of American common law. More important than pointing out these factors is pointing out the consequences of this deterioration, which are an overjudicialization of politics and an erosion of state power in favor of national authority. This study cannot come too soon given the ever-increasing role the judiciary plays in lives of Americans. In order to rectify the problems now associated with the judiciary it is necessary to understand what has led to this current predicament. While a systematic analysis of the transformation of the judiciary is a necessary step, it is also necessary to uncover the philosophical underpinnings of this development in order to confront the arguments which have enabled the development.

In order to reach an understanding of the political implications associated with the American common law system I employ empirical methods in chapters 3–5. I use the American states as the basis for a comparative analysis in order to discern what political and social factors influence the development of certain common law characteristics. These characteristics include: uncodified law, the definition of crime, sentencing, methods of pleading, the jury, and the divide between law and equity. In chapter 3 I use an event history analysis to study state adoption patterns of reforms associated with commerce, crime, sentencing, and methods pleading. Through this approach I am able to relate certain social and political factors to the commitment a state has to various common law principles. In order to study juries at the state level I use a time series approach in chapter 4 to show what factors influence the percentage of jury trials in a state. This chapter sheds some light on why the use of juries in both criminal and civil trials has been on the decline. Chapter 5 deals with the divide between courts of law and equity at the state and national level by providing a critical review of federal court decisions. Chapter 5 shows that courts have made decisions which have distorted the divide between law and equity, a divide which is essential for a common law system to function properly.

The final chapter deals with the philosophical origins of the American common law tradition in an effort to show that the dismantling of the American common law is the result of a philosophical tradition, not random events. Chapter 6 deals primarily with Montesquieu, Blackstone, and Hamilton; it shows that the common law system was compromised when it became integrated with liberalism.

This study seeks to reclaim a lost tradition. Even if America is unable to reclaim this tradition perhaps scholars will come to recognize the importance of this tradition, as a legitimizing force and consensus building mechanism at the time of the American founding. This becomes important when one expands one's vision beyond American shores and focuses on newly democratizing nations and begins to ask what institutions and social forces must be in place in order for democracy to develop. While this question is not new, it can certainly be reframed. In understanding our own founding, we can hypothesize, and then study, how institutions can be arranged to integrate and maintain local customs and traditions in order to foster the growth of a stable government which protects liberty.

1

Defining the Common Law and Surveying the Literature

When governments are initially formed there is a concern about legitimacy. Without a sound basis on which to stand, a government may never get off the ground. Establishing laws that provide safety and order is the first job of a government so that the society knows what the boundaries are. Common law provided a source of legitimacy and served as a stabilizing force for the new colonies and later for states that entered the union. The common law was a system of law that had been around since the eleventh century in England and was based on customs, tradition, and history. The common law was transmitted through judicial precedent, but the people came to know it through tradition and customs. This trend carried over to the new colonies since the settlers had no other laws than the ones they brought over from England. The new laws and constitutions, such as the Mayflower Compact, had groundings in the common law tradition. Once an initial system was established and the primary guidelines were understood, a government may then move beyond common law and enact new laws, but since no government can address all concerns, the common law would continue to serve as a stabilizing force as it could be consulted as a guide for dealing with new events that no statutes yet addressed. It would be difficult to imagine an omnipotent legislature that could foresee all problems and pass legislation accordingly. The judiciary, as it institutionalized custom, tradition, and history, was relied on to fill in where the legislature left gaps.

Why legal scholars have an interest in common law is obvious; since the nation's founding it has been the central branch of how law develops and how the judiciary works. Not only is common law a collection of laws, but it also places restrictions on judicial behavior, such as consulting precedent and using juries. The legal profession has, until fairly recently, been defined by the common law. Such institutions as the bar and methods of pleading are grounded in the common law. But common law has been changed and its impact has been diminished, which has led to decreased interest by legal scholars. Political scientists would benefit from joining the discussion on common law precisely when the common law has begun to deteriorate. The change in common law encompasses questions about the relative sphere of judicial authority, and as the hallmarks of common law have traditionally defined that sphere, political scientists might be interested in knowing how judicial authority has changed as a result of a change in common law. While common law places quite a bit of authority into the hands of judges to discover law, it also places quite a few restrictions on the power they can wield and the latitude they have in making decisions. If the common law deteriorates, so too do those mechanisms that restrict judicial authority. Furthermore, what are the ramifications for federalism and the separation of powers when there is a judiciary which is no longer steeped in common law traditions or restrained by the traditional mechanisms of common law?

Political scientists and legal scholars have typically treated the common law as a historical artifact, that is to say, interesting, but not crucial for our understanding of modern politics. There are components of the common law which have received more attention than others; specifically precedent and juries, but these studies have taken place outside the context of common law. Both political scientists and legal scholars have spent time studying these two hallmarks of common law, but legal scholars have given more attention to the common law, until recently. In the past decade there have been a few notable studies by political scientists which focus on common law and its role in American political development. These studies have come at a time when interest by legal scholars has begun to wane. Since interest by the legal community has faded as the common law has faded, it is important for another field to pick up its study. Not only is political science capable of making new insights with regard to common law and its role in the nation's founding, but also what the modification of the common law means to our current political environment. It is my contention that the political impact of the common law has been underestimated by legal scholars, and political scientists have ignored the crucial role the modification of the common law has played in American political development. The deterioration of the common law has led to fewer restraints on the judiciary and national government, making possible a transition to a more centralized and judiciary-centered political scheme. The new understanding of common law is judge-made law, whereas the original understanding was judge-discovered law. While it is a subtle distinction, the distinction is crucial to an understanding of what it means to move from a common law system to one dominated by positivism. This will be a theme that will be addressed in all chapters of this project.

In addition to providing a new outlook with respect to common law, I provide two methodological improvements for looking at the common law. First, legal scholars typically rely on a case study method or historical investigation; I will employ quantitative methods of inquiry seeking to bring a more systematic understanding of common law with results that provide more breadth than what has been previously available. Second, I seek to provide a more comprehensive understanding of common law and its implications than what political science has thus far been able to provide by employing a multimethod approach that will provide relevant findings for quantitative and nonquantitative political scientists alike.

This first chapter will provide an overview of the relevant literature by both legal scholars and political scientists. Through a review of the literature I will not only be able to show where my study fits in with the existing literature, but where it adds to the literature. There are some basic questions which will guide this review. What does empirical political science know of the common law? Why has empirical political science, to this point, not focused on common law in its entirety? Should political science consider common law more seriously? What can political science learn from what legal scholars have found? What could legal scholars learn if they were to apply the methodological rigor of empirical political science? These questions will provide an introduction to the field of common law study which will lead to a better understanding of why it is important.

SECTION I: WHAT POLITICAL SCIENTISTS KNOW

As noted in the introduction, the primary areas of concern for political scientists, with regard to common law, are precedent and juries. This section will treat both topics separately. Within the topic of precedent, studies by legal scholars will also be discussed in order to give a more comprehensive picture of what is known about the topic.

Section I A: Precedent

The belief that precedents guided the decisions of judges was brought into question by political scientists in the early 1960s. Notable political scientists, such as Robert Dahl, recognized that there was something else at work that motivated judges' decisions other than precedent. The attitudinal model, rational choice scholars, and institutionalists all provide insight into how judges make their decisions if their decisions are understood not to be completely restrained by precedent. What follows is a brief review of these scholars, particularly the attitudinalists and the institutionalists, who have contributed to the understanding of how judges use precedent in their decisions, and what motivates them to abandon precedent in some cases.

In stark contrast to the legalistic approach to studying judicial behavior, the attitudinal model contends that "judges decide disputes in light of the facts of the case, given their ideological attitudes and values" (Segal and Spaeth 2002, 231). Decisions are reached not by ignoring facts, but by judges interpreting facts based on their individual preferences. If there are two components of the legalistic model—true meaning and precedent—the attitudinal model argues that true meaning is unknowable and repudiates the influence of precedent. Early attitudinal scholars found support for their claims when they found that many lower court judges refused to follow Supreme Court precedents (Peltason 1961; Tarr 1977). The legalist approach does not focus on the political leanings or predispositions of the judges, but explains judicial decisions based on the legal facts of the case and the precedents that the current case rests on.

To some degree, casual observation of the appointment process of federal judges would lead one to believe that judges do not make decisions which are strictly guided by the law. No matter how ardently Hamilton argues on behalf of the nonpolitical nature of the courts (*Federalist* 78), the fact remains that Article II, Section 2 of the Constitution would not have been included unless the founders understood that even individuals making decisions in a non-elected position can be influenced by politics.

> To the extent that the legal model requires justices to find the "correct" answer to legal questions, it should not matter much whom the President nominates or whether the Senate confirms, given a requisite modicum of legal training and intelligence (Segal and Spaeth 2002, 178)

This position might be a bit overstated, but the authors get their point across that discounting the impact of politics and attitudes on justices' decisions is inaccurate and possibly naïve.

Schubert (1964) formulated one of the earliest attitudinal approaches, in addition to his work developing other approaches within the behavioral school. He, and others, were influenced by, and built upon, what the legal realists (Llewellyn 1931) had initiated; a model that rejected the notion that judges made their decisions in a vacuum devoid of any internal or external influences. Schubert essentially placed strict and loose constructionists into ideology spaces dependent upon the case being decided. Schubert developed a scheme to show that case stimuli and the values of a justice could be placed on an ideological scale. He then established "ideal points" for justices to show their general levels of liberalism or conservatism in relation to other justices and cases.

The attitudinal model has been challenged by institutional explanations. Institutional explanations were made popular, but quickly abandoned, by Robert G. McCloskey in *The American Supreme Court*. The strongest evidence for the attitudinal model is found at the Supreme Court level, and has been reported by Lee Epstein and Gary King (2002) in response to legal scholars who argue that precedent is the strongest influence on Supreme Court justices. But since the Supreme Court handles only a small fraction of the total caseload in the United States, and since it has a unique institutional setting, the Supreme Court findings may be an anomaly and not the rule.

The prominence of the attitudinal model seemingly stymied the development of alternate paradigms until quite recently. The release of a volume by Cornell Clayton and Howard Gillman has brought institutionalism back *en vogue* with judicial scholars, building on the earlier work of Robert G. McCloskey. Institutionalists agree that the attitudes of judges are not to be ignored, but argue that the institutional arrangement of the judiciary, from within and with regard to the other branches, are factors which have the most influence on the decisions of judges. The most productive research has been at the state level since the institutional variations between states provide a comparative analysis that is difficult to find at the national level (Hall and Brace 1994; Brace and Hall 1995; Brace and Hall 1993; Langer 2002). It is almost as if the states provide the conditions for a natural experiment. The findings by the institutionalists have led to some revisions of the attitudinal model findings (Clayton and Gillman 1999). It is now believed that the attitudes of judges are not the primary factor in deciding cases at all levels.

With this said, there has been little effort to test what allows the judges to stray from precedent, and what the effects are when they do. Chapter 5 of this manuscript looks at both of these questions when I examine Supreme Court cases decided in equity rather than law. While I do not pay special attention to precedent per se, an examination of equity necessitates that one look to the alternatives that are before the judges when they make their decisions. Chapter 5 will not resolve any differences between the attitudinalists and the institutionalists but will provide evidence that both circumstance and political outlook are important variables in judges' decisions. But what I add to the debate is an answer to what can happen when precedent is abandoned. In the equity cases I deal with, the majority decision ignores controlling precedent and makes a decision based on their own reasoning of the case facts with no consultation with past cases with similar facts. I conclude that this has created confusion over where the division between law and equity is, and what power the court has in defining the distinction.

Section I B: Juries

Article III, Section 2 and Amendment VI of the U.S. Constitution clearly state that jury trials are to be utilized in both civil and criminal trials. Like most constitutional matters there is no dispute over what the text says, but there is disagreement over the meaning and what the practical implications are. Recently, the use of jury trials has decreased in an effort to increase the efficiency and decrease the cost associated with trials.[1] Jury trials have been supplanted by bench trials and alternative forms of dispute resolution, such as plea-bargaining and arbitration. As a result, there have been those who oppose the trend away from jury trials, and there have been those who defend it. Those who defend the trend find support in Supreme Court cases which have authorized the use of non-jury methods of case disposition. Jury trial supporters argue that juries are the only means by which to ensure a fair trial, and a means that is guaranteed by the Constitution (Landsman 1999; DiPrima 1995). Those who support the trend away from jury trials say that justice can be better served without juries, who are prone to discrimination and emotional decisions (Butler 1995; Lettow 1994; King 1993). They continue, the use of alternative means of resolution provide a more efficient and cheaper court system which makes it accessible to more people (Alschuler 1979; Langbein 1979; Langbein 1992).

While there have been calls for increased use of juries, there seems to be a resignation among scholars that reinstituting the jury is a lost cause. Now research tends to focus not on whether or not the jury system should be employed, but what happens when the jury is employed. One area that receives quite a bit of attention is jury discrimination. While justice is blind, juries may not be. Researchers worry that jurors who possess racist or sexist attitudes may be swayed by factors other than the facts of the case (Curran 1983; Schafran 1990; Wikler 1980; Butler 1995). Most of these studies have found that discriminatory attitudes do permeate the decision process of jurors. There are studies that focus on the discriminatory attitudes of judges, but the results of those studies are inconclusive (Hemmens et al. 1998).

A second area of research is centered on how jurors make their decisions by creating what researchers like to call decision models. Researchers seek to understand what factors influence jurors other than the facts (Gershman 1986; Steele and Thornburg 1991; Levine 1996; Hartmus and Levine 1998). What most research has found is that juries typically make the correct decision. Dino Gerardi concludes from his study that individual jurors have a high probability of making the correct decision, but that the unanimity rule benefits the defendant who is guilty. Under the unanimity rule the guilty party is more likely not to be convicted, but under rules of nonunanimity the jury gets the correct verdict with a probability approaching one (Gerardi 2000). A separate study, done by researchers at the California Institute of Technology, finds roughly the same results as Gerardi (2000) but that jurors in a nonunanimous setting are more likely to act strategically, and therefore the probability of a correct verdict decreases, but is still greater than in a unanimous setting. But the researchers agree that the guilty defendant is benefited under the unanimity rule since juries are less likely to convict when forced to be unanimous (Guarnaschelli et al. 2000). These studies were performed in criminal settings, and similar studies deal with civil disputes. In civil disputes, where fiscal rewards are given, there is more variability in the decisions handed down by juries. Even in cases with similar facts, there can be a large degree of variability (McCaffery et al. 1995). While this may give ammunition to those who support a movement away from juries, there needs to be a focus on what this means when looked at in a common law context. If the juries are awarding different amounts, and the variation occurs not within a jurisdiction, but between jurisdictions, then the idea behind the jury as community conscience may be correct after all, and some solace may be found in these findings.

While jury researchers are also interested in such things as sentencing patterns (Sauer 1995; Lanni 1999), this review provides an accurate account of what is being studied. The research cited provides valuable information into the workings of juries, but it lacks an appreciation for the larger issues which surround juries. First, juries were intended to be a reflection of the community's interest, and a reflection of its conscience. There has been no research conducted which seeks an understanding of how well the community's interest is represented in non-jury trial settings.[2] Second, there has been little investigation into what has caused the decrease in jury trials. While the common explanation is workload, there has been no study which employs a large number of judicial jurisdictions to test the workload hypothesis. Finally, there seems to be little concern over what it means for juries to have a less prominent role. The theory of juries implies that they provide a buffer between government, law, and the people in an effort to preserve liberty; but there has been no study which tests whether or not there has been a deterioration of this buffer as the role of the jury decreases. By looking through the lens of common law, one is able to see the far-reaching implications of juries. Chapter 4 of this manuscript will provide insight into the three areas I have outlined. Chapter 4 focuses on civil and criminal juries at the state level in a time-series design from 1976–2002. Chapters 2 and 4 will provide a more thorough description of the research design. Chapter 4 is designed to show what factors have led to the decline in jury use, and if there is validity to the workload thesis.

SECTION II: WHAT LEGAL SCHOLARS KNOW

Legal scholars should receive credit for the attention they have paid to common law. Legal scholars notice that there has been a modification in our understanding of common law, though what has caused this change and when it occurred is up for debate. There are two factors, equity and codification, that receive attention as being involved in the modification of American common law. Some scholars might cite equity and codification as manifestations of deeper societal changes, whereas others attribute moves toward codification and uniting law and equity as the primary reasons why common law has been compromised (McDowell 1982; Nelson 1994; Cook 1981). While it cannot be shown in this review which way the causation arrow points, or settle the dispute between the two camps, I will make the argument for both sides and show how this study will bring some resolution to the debate.

Section II A: Equity

Equity almost seems a foreign term, especially to political scientists. It is rare that anyone raises objection to the unification of law in equity in our courts, or cites the Judiciary Act of 1789 that provides the distinction. As it was originally understood, equity was distinct from law, and was a system of jurisprudence that was, as Lord Bacon assessed, "ordained to supply the deficiencies of the common law." The purpose of equity courts was to extend a statute that did not directly deal with a particular case or to omit cases that the text of the statute did directly relate to but would require a treatment more harsh than the intent of the statute would require. To grasp some sense of how equity was originally conceived, it is appropriate to cite sixteenth-century English case law. In *Eyston v. Studd* (1574) Plowden writes:

> It is not the words of the law, but the internal sense of it that makes the law, and our law (like all others) consists of two parts, viz. body and soul, the letter of the law is the body of the law, and the sense and reason of the law is the soul of the law, *quia ratio legis est anima legis*. . . . And it often happens that when you know the letter, you know not the sense, for sometimes it is more large and extensive. And equity, which in Latin is called *equitas*, enlarges or diminishes the letter. (75 Eng. Rep. 688, 2 Plowden 460, 464)

This quote reflects not only the need for equity in the court in order to achieve justice, but for the separation of courts of law and equity in order to protect the rule of law. Lord Coke brings to light the power that equity gives to judges, and their ability to decide what the legislature intended by their statutes and in effect giving judges in equity the final legislative authority.

> A construction made by the judges, that cases out of the letter of a statute, yet being within the same mischiefe, or cause of the making of the same, shall be within the same remedie that the statute provideth: and the reason here of is, that for the lawmakers could not possibly set downe all cases in expresse terms. (Coke 1628)

And while not a comprehensive definition of equity, these two citations give a general idea of what the original conception was and why it was important to separate law and equity.[3]

While efforts were made to unite courts of law and equity in America at the end of the nineteenth century, real progress was not made until Roscoe Pound, the American Bar Association, and the other institutions manned by academics, judges, and law experts got on board during the early part of the twentieth century. It did not take long for legal scholars to take note of the changing landscape. As early as 1911, Henry Ingersoll wrote an article noting this change. Ingersoll begins by noting that the efforts of Hobbes in England were realized in America by David Dudley Field and those who followed his lead. His study focuses on the state courts and how they have transformed the line between law and equity. He breaks the courts into three categories: (1) states with separate courts of law and equity, (2) states where equity and law are distinct but in the same court, and (3) states where the distinction has been abolished. In 1911 there were only seven states that had separate courts of law and equity, and twenty-one total that recognized a distinction between the two. What Ingersoll lacks in his study, and surprisingly has not been corrected for, is an explanation of why certain courts chose their path and what it means for law in their particular state. In chapter 3 of this study I will add to Ingersoll's study when I provide a quantitative analysis of the pattern of the states' adoption of the Federal Rules of Civil Procedure, a reform which essentially eliminates common law pleading and further blurs the line between law and equity.

Of course more recent studies have been done. What these studies agree on is that the line of demarcation between courts of law and equity has blurred. What is clear now is that judges, especially federal judges, have the opportunity to "slip into the shoes of equity" when the law is insufficient for their means (Laycock 1993; Manning 2001; Surbin 1987). Even objections have been raised by scholars who notice that the courts of equity and law have been conjoined. John F. Manning writes "At the same time, the broad judicial lawmaking power implicit in the equity of the statute would potentially undermine the federalism objectives of bicameralism and presentment" (Manning 2001, 78). Proponents of the increased use of equity find that there is little choice. Douglas Laycock points out that codification has left little choice but to allow for more use of equity. Since statutes cannot take into account all of the various circumstances that may arise, equitable protection by the court is necessary to correct for the lack of existing common law. Those scholars who agree with Laycock see equity as a way of checking the legislature. And while these scholars do not cite the common law, this is the classic common law interpretation of what the court's role is, but this is not the common law conception of how equity and law are to be used, since the law served as a check on the judiciary, and when the two are combined, the judiciary has no check on it.

I build upon the existing research in chapter 5. Chapter 5 is designed to look at the effect court decisions made in equity have had on federalism and the separation of powers. Through an examination of these cases I will test the projections of both Manning (2001) and Laycock (1993), projections which mirror those of the Anti-Federalists and Federalists. To restate, Manning says that when law and equity are fused, there is a threat to the principles of federalism and the separation of powers, with the risk being a court with authority to override the states and the legislature. Laycock does not deny that this risk exists, but also says that the Supreme Court will not overstep its bounds, and simply provide a check on the legislature. Through an examination of some of the most cited cases of equity, clarity to this dispute will be found.

Section II B: Codification

The same efforts, and proponents, that brought about the unification of law and equity also brought about codification. While the history of this process is reserved for chapter 2 of this study, a review of the more recent literature will be helpful. Unfortunately for those interested in codification and its effects, there has not been much research; Mark D. Rosen makes the point that "a piecemeal codification of the bulk of the common law has occurred during the last sixty years, and, surprisingly, the academy has given hardly any attention to the consequences and wisdom of this recent switch" (Rosen 1994, 1119). Although this call to arms was made nearly a decade ago, little progress has been made. The first half of the twentieth century saw a lively debate over the implications of codification (Kadish 1978). This academic debate was interesting in the sense that it had practical implications. Advocates of codification began influencing policy makers, and the result was this country's second movement toward codification that began with the Federal Rules of Civil Procedure, through the Uniform Commercial Code, and continues through sentencing guidelines and the Penal Code.[4] What has been lost is the debate? It seems that those academics who opposed codification were lost in the transformation, and the critics of codification, or at least those who question it, have yet to find their way back. And while it is unfortunate that more research has not been given to codification, the work that has been done has provided some useful findings.

The opponents of codification were worried that there would be a bureaucratization of the law, a limitation of the adversarial system which would lead to limiting the jury, and would "advance an ethic of atomism at the expense of community solidarity" that the common law protected against (Rosen 1994). Furthermore, the common law provided a level of adaptability that some feared codification would be unable to replicate. Recent findings have shown that these warnings are in fact valid (Rosen 1994; Bodenheimer 1982). Codification has increased the level of bureaucratization of the law and may even be a cause for the declining use of juries. Judges also seem to have abandoned common law in favor of codified law. Even in areas that have not been directly addressed by codification efforts, common law is on the decline as a valid source of law due to the increased legitimacy afforded to code and statutes. And while these studies have provided important insights, no effort has been made to understand what the effects have been outside the courthouse, or what has prompted states to adopt various codified laws. Other research has been able to track the progress of various sections of codified law. Most of this research is of such a particular nature that it provides little external validity when its conclusions are applied to other areas of the law (Rosenthal 1978). I attempt to correct for these two shortcomings in chapter 3. In chapter 3, I perform an event history analysis on four areas of common law which were eventually codified: the Uniform Commercial Code, Federal Rules of Civil Procedure, Sentencing Guidelines, and Common Law Crime. Chapter 2 will give a fuller description of the research design and how each area applies to both common law and codification.

SECTION III: WHAT POLITICAL THEORY HAS BEEN DOING

While I have discussed political science, I have only focused on the quantitative camp. Political theorists have taken a new interest in the common law. This interest has been spurred by Professor James Stoner. Professor Stoner makes the argument that those who study the founding are in error when they omit a discussion of our common law foundations. He not only references the most prolific thinkers on both sides of the Atlantic at the time of the founding, but he examines the founding documents, specifically the Declaration of Independence and the Constitution. He points out that there are hallmarks of the common law in the Constitution, specifically in Article III and Amendment VI. But he also notes that many of the grievances against King George were violations of the common law (Stoner 1992 and 2003). Stoner continues, in his most recent volume, to explain how ignoring our common law foundations has permeated through the Supreme Court, therefore leading to many decisions that are in violation of the original spirit of the founding (Stoner 2003).

Stoner has influenced the work of others, including Paul O. Carrese in his recent volume, *The Cloaking of Power*. Professor Carrese does not focus entirely on the common law; he does spend quite a bit of energy focusing on how liberalism impacted the understanding of common law and constitutional government. Carrese concludes that the teaching of Montesquieu influenced Blackstone, and consequently Alexander Hamilton, which impacted the understanding of the judiciary at the time of the founding.

Chapter 6 of this manuscript will take up the argument of Stoner and Carrese. I will examine the thought of Montesquieu and Blackstone in relation to the argument of Hamilton in the *Federalist Papers*. The central thesis of this chapter focuses on Hamilton. Stoner and Carrese both overestimate the influence common law had on the thinking of Hamilton, which means, I argue, Hamilton was more closely aligned with Hobbes than Coke. Stoner and Carrese each note the transformation common law goes through when it encounters the liberalizing influences of Montesquieu and Blackstone, but underestimate the effect liberalism had on the thought of Hamilton. Hamilton is important in this discussion since he makes the most powerful arguments on behalf of the judiciary, and is the author of the *Federalist Papers*, which are most commonly cited by students of the judiciary. Therefore, the argument runs, the Anti-Federalists were correct in their assessment of the federal judiciary, and Hamilton saw the potential for power within the judiciary, and he was not opposed to this power in the hands of the judiciary. To state it a bit differently, the influence of Montesquieu and Blackstone can been seen most clearly in the thought of Hamilton, and it was Hamilton who was the chief proponent of the judiciary as it was constructed under the Constitution, and the judiciary is where we most clearly see the tendency to consolidate power, a direct result of its liberal roots.

Carrese and Stoner find at least one ally among legal scholars. Albert Alschuler (2000) writes about the deleterious effects the work of Oliver Wendell Holmes Jr. had on the law in general and the common law in particular. Both Carrese and Stoner see Holmes as a central force in transforming American law—a transformation that took American law away from its natural right foundation by adopting relativism. The work of all three is also complemented by the historical findings of Laurence Friedman and Morton Horowitz. I do not quarrel with the analysis of Holmes by Carrese, Stoner, or Alschuler. My primary objection to these studies is the amount of blame that is placed on Holmes. Without Montesquieu, Blackstone, and Hamilton there would be no Holmes. In other words, Holmes reaped what they sowed. Very rarely in politics, or any other walk of life, is there a punctuated equilibrium such as Carrese and Stoner make Holmes out to be. Even Alschuler tempers his thesis that Holmes is the pivotal figure in American law when he writes, "Lawyers that believe that judges before Holmes merely found law must have missed part of law school. They could not have read any opinion of Chief Justice Marshall" (Alschuler 2000, 96). Alschuler provides a brief discussion of Marshall's varying interpretations of the word *necessary*. Of course Carrese would combat this sentiment by stating that Marshall represented a true common law mind, not a legal positivist.

Relevant to the discussion of Hamilton is Gary L. McDowell's observation that, in the *Federalist Papers* written by Hamilton, "Montesquieu is invoked, but not Coke" (McDowell 1993, 396). Also, Coke is never invoked by Hamilton in his defense of the Bill of Rights or at the New York ratifying convention. According to McDowell, Hamilton's opinion of Coke was quite low. "For such a constitution Coke's medieval view of the common law was no longer necessary; indeed, it was no longer acceptable" (McDowell 1993, 399). These are peculiar facts that those who make Hamilton out as a common law mind have not confronted.

Even the most ardent critics of Holmes are able to recognize that it was the Enlightenment, of which Montesquieu was a part, that brought about reasoning from first principles and it was the common law that reasoned from the law as applied to the facts. James Q. Whitman points out that Coke was concerned with the laws of England, not law in general (Whitman 1991). Blackstone made a novel attempt to mingle reason and custom in his analysis of the law in a way that was quite different from Coke, who only referred to artificial reason, which is reason derived from a study of the law. Blackstone adapted eighteenth-century methodology and reason to medieval doctrines. As time progressed so too did Enlightenment principles which found a home in the American Constitution. The principles of Enlightenment were brilliantly articulated by Hamilton. Unfortunately for the common law this meant its impending doom in America. This book does not let Holmes off the hook, but instead suggests that Holmes was not the lone culprit.

In the final chapter of this book I make the argument that Holmes was not at all revolutionary, he merely learned the lessons of those who preceded him and at most applied those lessons in an unprecedented fashion. Chapter 6 does not dedicate much space to Holmes or Marshall. The focus is on Montesquieu, Blackstone, and Hamilton to show that these three thinkers indicate a strain of thought that runs counter to original common law principles and instead pushes for a judiciary which is active in the law-making process.

NOTES

1. According to the Bureau of Justice Statistics, 95 percent of felony convictions occur without a jury trial.

2. There has been research relating public opinion and the Supreme Court; there is no research that compares the ability of juries to judges.

3. A more comprehensive definition will be provided when equity in American Federal Courts is examined in chapter 5.

4. The first codification movement took place during the nineteenth century at the urging of David Dudley Field. Historians and legal scholars have spent some time studying this movement, but less attention has been paid to the movement in the twentieth century.

2

Debating the Common Law in America

This study does not join the debate over common law at its origins in Medieval Europe, but picks up with the ratification debates of the American Constitution. These debates, and the ones that follow, typify the disagreements over common law versus other forms of jurisprudence and law making. The arguments made by each side during the ratification debate did not end with the ratification of the U.S. Constitution but continued between Joseph Story and Andrew Jackson, through the debate surrounding the Codification Movement that followed in the beginning of the nineteenth century, and the argument over the enactment of uniform state laws. The intention of this study is to test the claims made by each side in order to help bring clarity to a debate that has taken place in this country since its founding. The empirical study begins in the middle of the twentieth century, so we must first go back to the nation's founding in order to have some grasp of what the current debate is over. This chapter is not an attempt to give a comprehensive history of American common law development, but will highlight the arguments of various generations in a way that shows consistency in the debate between generations.

While this study is mostly empirical, it would be a mistake to jump hastily into a description of the research design and all that is involved with that process. I must begin by sketching the arguments made by both sides of the debate during the ratification, and show how the arguments made by the Anti-Federalists and Federalists were adopted and built upon by those who debated these same issues during the movements to codify American common law. This will help uncover the issues that are central in the American understanding of law and its impact on such principles as liberty, community, and limited government. Furthermore, it is paramount to the empirical portion of this study to show a direct connection between the common law debates and the codification debates. The empirical study relies partly upon the reforms made during the codification movement to operationalize certain concepts of common law.

The first section of this chapter will proceed in three parts. First, I will revisit the ratification debates, paying particular attention to the arguments made by James Wilson and Publius, and the Anti-Federalist response. Second, I will show how this debate was picked up by Andrew Jackson and Joseph Story. It is in the Jackson-Story debates that we first witness a subtle change from common law to codification, and the evidence will be borne out. Finally, I will bring in the arguments of Jeremy Bentham, whose philosophy had a direct impact upon Americans who sought codification.

SECTION I: THE DEBATES

Section I A: The Federalists vs. Anti-Federalists

Before an account of the debates can be given, a definition of the common law must be established. But the initial problem faced in this project is in developing a working definition of common law. The very nature of common law almost wants to defy precise definition since one of its key characteristics is adaptability. However, there are some easily identifiable characteristics that may aid in the definition. Common law exists wherever precedents are used to identify law. This is quite different from Oliver Wendell Holmes's formulation. Holmes considers common law to be judge-made law. So, therefore, precedents create common law. The more traditional approach says that precedents reveal common law. Precedents are used as a guide to indicate to judges what the previous path has been, as justice demands that similar cases be treated in similar ways. Judges in the common law tradition do not make law; they discover it through a systematic search and application of precedent.

The common law also requires the use of juries. Juries must be drawn from the general community. A jury randomly selected from the community is the best representation of the community's sense of right and wrong. The jury must be allowed to find fact and apply the law. This formulation is consistent with what James Stoner says is part of the essence of common law. "Common law emphasizes assent rather than domination, the community rather than the state, moral authority rather than physical power" (Stoner 2003, 8).

The common law is not rigid; it is adaptable, just as the community that it is derived from has changing needs and considerations. Thus, codification is contrary to common law. While revision of statutes is possible, it violates what is at the essence of common law. Furthermore, common law decisions reflect the sentiment of the community; common law must be made locally in order to reflect this sentiment as the national stage is too far removed from the people to be truly responsive. Judges must be able, with the aid of the jury, to hand down decisions which best serve the interests of the community. While not all laws are defined under this system, traditionally those laws left undefined by the legislature are left for the courts and the community to define through tradition, practice, and history. Lastly, the common law is not positive law. It relies on the belief that a moral sense of right and wrong is possessed by each individual in a community. It has a natural law foundation. This conceptualization of law is quite different from the statutory outlook. Common law understands that the role of law is to be representative of the people, held accountable by the people, and be willed by the people in such a way that promotes the common good.

The Federalist position on common law is best seen in the thought of James Wilson, an important figure in the creation of the Constitution and ardent supporter of its ratification in Pennsylvania. While serving as professor of jurisprudence at the College of Philadelphia he gave a lecture entitled "Of the Common Law." In his lecture he made explicit his position on the subject. Wilson agreed that common law was necessary because of man's fallibility. Because man was fallible he could not be trusted as judge in his own case. For Wilson, men could not be trusted as judges in their own cases because there was a conflict in the different means men chose for arriving at justice. Furthermore, it was unlikely that the end product of what justice looked like could be agreed upon.

> To select and ascertain those means is often a matter of very considerable difficulty. Doubts may arise; opposite interests may occur; and the preference must be given to one side from a small overbalance, and from very nice views. This is particularly the case in questions with regard to justice. (Wilson 1967, 137)

This position is a departure from the English and medieval doctrine of common law (Hogue 1986). Common law was initially grounded in natural law. In the natural law formulation, man had an intuitive sense of right and wrong. The common law, for Wilson, took the place of this intuitive sense that he found lacking in men. For Wilson, "man was not able to make a decision regarding justice, but collectively, justice could be achieved, and this is where the common law came in" (Wilson 1967, 356). Common law was not only a collection of men drawn together to make decisions, according to Wilson, but a collection of practices and customs that had come to be followed and adopted by successive generations. But while there is little doubt that tradition and custom each play a central role in determining what the common law is, Wilson neglects the role of conscious reason. He neglects the role played by judges and lawyers who spend considerable time studying the law and trying to come to a conclusion that stays consistent with both the needs of the community and with what has transpired in the past. Wilson abandons this deliberative process as well as natural law as principles necessary for common law. To put it another way, Wilson reconstructs common law theory to meet his own needs by abandoning the original understanding. He believed that there could be no natural law basis because the common law had to be changing and mutable. But Wilson overestimated the restrictiveness of natural law. Adaptability is not necessarily inconsistent with natural law, as Wilson believed. The fact that circumstances change does not mean natural law changes, but instead natural law remains a force that can be consulted when confronted with new challenges. By removing the natural law foundations from common law, Wilson laid a foundation for an all-out assault on common law by later generations. Wilson probably would not have approved of the assault on common law since he was, at least on the surface, a proponent of the common law.

When examined closely there are contradictions in Wilson's thought. First, common law without natural law is not common law. By extracting natural law from common law, Wilson extracted the foundation of common law which made it possible and defensible. Second, for Wilson, men who cannot be trusted on their own can be trusted as a collective. Men who are to be restrained because they lack an intuitive sense of right and wrong are capable of bringing about concepts of justice through competition and tradition. Wilson's argument is similar to the argument made by Publius in the *Federalist Papers*, which means the contradictions in Wilson's thought are also present in the thought of Publius. The consensus among the Federalists seems to be that government is necessary because the actions of men will not always conform to the dictates of reason (*Federalist* 15), and in *Federalist* 10 we see the claim that an enlightened statesman will not always be at the helm.[1] The Federalists believed that the surest way to liberty was through stability, and by citing failures of past confederacies they arrived at the conclusion that the surest way to stability is through a "partly-federal, partly-national" system (*Federalist* 39). Therefore, as the Federalists argued, in order to provide stability one could not have a confederacy (federation); one needed something with a stronger central government. Madison made his position clear at the Constitutional Convention by citing examples from Greece and Shay's Rebellion. Madison was in favor of, as were the other Federalists, a strengthened national government that had the ability to provide stability so that liberty could be preserved. The point is made throughout the *Federalist Papers* that factions (which are harmful to government) originate at the local level, and the national government provides the remedy. Even the last of the papers makes this point:

> The additional securities to republican government, to liberty, and to property, to be derived from the adoption of the plan, consist chiefly in the restraints which the preservation of the union will impose upon local factions and insurrections, and upon the ambition of powerful individuals in single states. (*Federalist* 85, 452–53)[2]

What the thought of Publius, and his defense of a strengthened central government, shares with Wilson, and his formulation of common law, is that the virtue of the people alone cannot be trusted. Furthermore, the system that both Publius and Wilson[3] support takes some of the authority and decision-making power away from the community where the problem originates and where the solution will have the most direct impact. For Publius, stability can only be attained by having an energetic national government that has the authority to limit factions.

Through the centralizing tendencies in the thought of the Federalists one can see the objections they raise to common law thought. Even while Madison (one-third of Publius) in the *Virginia Resolutions* argues that the federal courts do not have common law authority, but the state courts alone retain such authority, he makes an argument for limiting the sphere in which common law authority can be claimed. Furthermore, the efforts of Publius, and Madison specifically in *Federalist* 10, in *Federalist* 39 show that much is to be gained by putting more authority in the hands of the national government. And according to Madison, the national government does not have common law jurisdiction. So by logical extension, moving matters to the national scene where common law does not exist (or should not) is the same as saying that common law should no longer be consulted as a source of relevant authority on matters of justice. Publius, in *Federalist* 78–83, argues that the federal court system is more beneficial to the general welfare than the state courts. But the federal court structure, especially the structure of the appellate courts, violates nearly every principle of common law courts. They are far removed from the people geographically and in spirit—meaning they are not required to be representative of the community's interests—there is no assurance of trial by jury at the appellate level, and issues of law and equity are conjoined in the federal system. So whether or not the federal courts were given authority over common law issues makes little difference in their being defined as common law courts, since absent in the federal structure are those mechanisms necessary for establishing a common law system. This leads one to conclude that although the Federalists do not explicitly state their opposition to common law, or perhaps are unaware of the consequences to common law under the system they support, the Federalist position is, by careful analysis, opposed to common law. Even in decisions on the Alien and Sedition Acts, the courts were not truly settling common law matters; they were making decisions on statutes.

The complications this introduced into the judicial structure can be seen in the response of the Anti-Federalists. Morton Horwitz makes the point that the Federalist position transforms the common law into a basis for jurists "to conceive of the common law as an instrument of will" (Horwitz 1977, 22). Herbert Storing cites two fundamental considerations from the Anti-Federalists which establish the basis of their position: (1) only a small republic can enjoy a voluntary attachment of the people to the government and a voluntary obedience to the laws and (2) only a small republic can secure the government to the people" (Storing 1981b, 16). Knowing their position with regard to the proper size of a state will help highlight their position on the common law. For the Anti-Federalists the rules that dictate the policy process will determine, in the Anti-Federalist view, whether or not the resulting policy decision is in the public good. The process is just as important as the outcome in achieving the public good. And for the Anti-Federalists, the public good is determined by each local community determining what is in its own best interest, because the local community is more familiar with the needs and values of its citizens than a centralized government overseeing a large number of communities. The logic of this formulation is that the community shares certain values and goals which lead them to a higher level of agreement concerning the public good than what can be achieved in a larger society (*Agrippa VIII*, cited in Storing 1981a). Even with this short foray into Anti-Federalist thought, it should be apparent where they stand on common law and why.

Though there were a number of writers who are classified as Anti-Federalists, there are a collection of writers who most aptly characterize their most prominent positions. And while each of the authors may differ on the particulars, the fundamental belief that the scale of the government is as important as the institutions that make it up is the basis for the thought of the Anti-Federalists. For instance, McClaine from North Carolina expressed his concern over what he saw as the consolidating tendency of the Constitution—and the problem of consolidating communities that did not share the same interests.

> But, sir, it is clear that a consolidation is intended. . . . It is too large. . . . I conceive that, in the present case, a consolidated government can by no means suit the genius of the people. . . . We see plainly that men who come from New England are different from us. They are ignorant of our situation; they do not know the state of our country. They cannot with safety legislate us. (Elliot 1941, 24)

And it was not only Southerners who shared this concern; James Winthrop of Massachusetts said that:

> The idea of an uncompounded republick [sic], on an average of one thousand miles in length, and eight hundred in breadth, and containing six million white inhabitants all reduced to the same standard of morals, of habits, and of laws, is in itself an absurdity, and contrary to the whole experience of mankind. (Ford 1970, 63)

Winthrop's outlook seems to stem from his belief expressed in *Agrippa VII* that the primary bond of government is self-interest. He follows this argument to say that local interests are the most closely connected to self-interest; therefore the citizen's bond is stronger at the local level since the same interests are shared. Decisions should be made through deliberation within the community. They should be made at the level closest to the people.

In his writings, Brutus objects to the Constitution's adoption on various grounds, but when it comes to the judiciary he is concerned, as he is with the two other branches, that it can easily usurp its specified powers and serve as a force that will also usurp the authority of the states. Brutus argues that the state governments should be responsible for nearly all domestic matters and the administration of justice. His concern is that, geographically speaking, the general government is too far removed from the people, and substantively speaking, the representatives elected to office cannot adequately represent the varied interests of the population due to the ratio of representative to people and the way in which the districts are constructed. For these reasons, Brutus concludes that the members of government are excessively insulated from the general public and may pursue their own agenda with little consequence. This is why Brutus argues for states to retain control over their affairs as they are more manageable and accountable to the people due to their size. In fact, Brutus argues that the local communities should be consulted even before the state governments. Brutus bluntly states that:

> provision is to be made for the administration of justice in the respective states. . . . The peace and happiness of a community is as intimately connected with the prudent direction of their domestic affairs, and the due administration of justice among themselves [the states], as with a competent provision for their defense against foreign invaders, and indeed more so. (Ketcham 1986, 287)

Brutus meticulously examines the Constitution phrase by phrase and draws out possible implications of each phrase. The general conclusion he reaches is that the separation of powers is insufficient and that the state powers allotted by the Constitution are insufficient to stop the national government from growing beyond its intended sphere. Furthermore, the men and the institutions are not separated enough from the law. Whoever is in power has complete control over the law and may interpret and change it as they see fit. And given that the institutions (especially the courts since their members are unelected with life tenure) are properly insulated from the public, consent from the governed is often not needed.

The principles of common law offer valid solutions to Brutus's critique of the system constructed by the men in Philadelphia. For one there is a jury. A jury, if properly chosen, is representative of the community therefore ensuring that the governed have some say in the outcome.[4] Second, the judges are restricted by precedent, history, and custom. If the judges abandon precedent, history, or custom, they will be held accountable by the community they are in close proximity with. Third, since the judge is a member of the community that he makes decisions in, it is likely that he has similar interests to the members of that community. The common law system addresses each of Brutus's concerns by providing representation, institutional restrictions, and accountability. Whether Brutus had the common law in mind as the proper solution cannot be concluded from his writings during the ratification debates, but by properly aligning his concerns with the principles of common law, it is easy to see a connection between his concerns and the solution a common law system provides.

Section I B: The Early Republic

After the new government had taken hold, the idea of where the common law stood was still undecided. The new debate was over whether the common law was integrated into the Constitution, especially with respect to crime, and whether the federal judiciary had jurisdiction in matters of common law. Even before the end of the decade, the Jeffersonian Republicans feared that the judiciary had begun to consider themselves on par with the legislature in terms of governing and promoting law (Horwitz 1977, 30). They attributed the growing power of the judiciary to the practice of hearing cases of common law by the federal judiciary and the resulting decisions which tended to carry as much weight as national legislation. The Federalist position was that the judiciary was acting just as it should, not surprising given the high number of Federalist judges that sat on the courts. The issue first came to a head through open debate of the Alien and Sedition Acts. Despite the obvious objections to the Alien and Sedition Acts as a violation of the Bill of Rights, the Republicans were angered at the expansive power they gave to the courts.

> Beyond the more obvious problems the Alien and Sedition Acts presented to the Bill of Rights, they were being justified by the Federalists on the basis of common law, which they held had been carried over even after the Constitution had been ratified. (McDowell 1982, 56)

There ensued a debate over whether the language of Article III, which gives the federal courts their power, was restrictive or expansive, and whether common law was under the jurisdiction of federal judges. Thomas Jefferson, a Republican, argued that to deduce that the common law was a part of the Constitution was logically flawed. He argued that the Constitution laid the foundation for all laws that followed, and therefore no law in the United States could precede it in time. The only laws which were valid were those that became law through the system established by the U.S. Constitution. Since common law existed prior to the Constitution through custom and precedent and not through the Constitution, it could not be considered constitutional or under the jurisdiction of the federal courts, which could only speak on constitutional matters. For Jefferson and other Republicans, the only hope for preserving liberty was a strict adherence to the letter of the law. The common law was uncertain and open to influence by the national legislature and court system that could, through manipulation of the common law, create a system of government that would take away states' rights and consolidate power at the national level.

The Federalists, on the other hand, read more broadly the language of the constitution and the implications of Article III. They inferred from the necessary and proper clause that Congress could make laws concerning seditious libel, making it a constitutional law with implications on the constitution, and if this is true, then Article III, which states that the court has authority "arising under the constitution," concludes that federal courts do have jurisdiction. The Federalists were accused of expanding the sphere of the national government beyond the bounds that a strict construction of the Constitution would allow. The Federalist defense was that in order to follow the Constitution, one must read into it the intentions and reasoning of the founders. Since at this time the Federalists had a strong foothold in the national government, it served their interests to expand its authority.

The debate ended with a Republican victory, but the common law had taken a blow. While I have not attempted to give a full review of the episode considered above, what I have shown will allow me to draw attention to a few pertinent developments. First, law as it was discussed in this context was a power struggle between political elites. The laws passed were detrimental to one party but beneficial to another and this brought the issue to the forefront, not the concern for justice. Second, we see that both sides have seemingly abandoned common law as a part of the federal government. While the Republicans argue that it has no place in the federal structure, the Federalists support its transformation into statutes. While the Federalists may seem favorable to common law through their integration of it through legislation, this process is destructive to common law. The measures taken by each side were damaging to the common law, for even those who sought to preserve common law wanted to do so only through revising it. By integrating it into the system through statute, or by relegating it to the states where it could be overruled by federal courts, the common law was now at risk of being lost entirely, especially after its natural law foundation had been stripped away. After the debate ended over the Alien and Sedition Acts, the debate over common law receded into the background until the 1820s when a codification movement swept through America.

Section I C: Codification Movement

The Codification Movement sought to end future debate over American jurisprudence by bringing more certainty to the law by making it less subjective and more restricted by statutes. The object was to depoliticize the law, which would lead to more certainty. This movement had its beginnings with James Wilson and others who eradicated natural law principles from the common law, thus making it less authoritative and more open to change and revision. Part of the objective was not only to make the law more stable and certain, but to make it more easily understood by the public and law professionals as well.

John Milton Goodenow wrote a treatise entitled *Historical Sketches of the Principles and Maxims of American Jurisprudence* that argued for a more systematic form of law that would eliminate the uncertainty and variability in common law. Goodenow did not want to eliminate common law, but wanted to update the common law system so that it could be preserved.[5] Goodenow continued the tradition initiated by Wilson by systematically eliminating the natural law foundations of the common law. Wilson continued to cling to the idea that man had some binding moral sense, even though he thought it could not be trusted, but Goodenow denied that any moral sense of right and wrong existed in man. Goodenow concluded that men perceived God and justice in different ways, and it was these differences that made necessary a systematic form of law that left little room for discretion and interpretation" (Goodenow 1819, 4–33). While Wilson's message was a bit more palatable, the two men still arrived at the same conclusion. Both agree that men in the public differ over what is right and wrong which leads to the need for government and law; where Goodenow says that a binding moral sense does not exist, Wilson says that the binding moral sense is present but varies between individuals, thus weakening its binding force.

David Dudley Field was the first to take positive action in an effort to codify common law. He began his movement in New York, seeking to pass reforms at the state level. While he did not achieve his goal of bringing about complete codification, he did lay the groundwork for future efforts. The states that had been around the longest resisted his reforms, and those states that came into the Union later and did not have a strong English settlement rapidly adopted Field's reforms, otherwise known as the Field Code.

As was seen with Field, this debate was not relegated to a strictly theoretical forum; this debate was played out in the political arena. When Andrew Jackson took office, he continued the Republican tradition and sought to limit national government and increase the democratic features of the American system. Jackson feared the nationalizing influence of the judiciary and sought to limit its authority. The nationalism of Story and the grass roots democracy of Jackson were the source of conflict between the two men. Their disagreement over the role of government is seen in the debate over common law and the judiciary. Jackson looked at the judiciary and judicial discretion with great disregard. Judicial discretion is at the heart of common law. Jackson sought the passage of laws, through the legislature, which were in accord with a strict construction of the Constitution. Jackson sought the codification of laws that had previously been considered unreliable and subjective since they were part of a system that did not adhere solely to written law. By codifying laws, through the creation of a more statute-oriented system of law, Jackson sought to rein in the powers of the judiciary by limiting its discretion, which was the source of much of their power. This, according to Jackson's calculations, would place more power in the hands of the democratically elected legislature, thus giving more power to the people.

Story was opposed to codification, and the sole reason was not that he was concerned with his own shrinking authority as a judge. Story's understanding of the law was that it was something more, something deep rooted and sincere, than mere positive decrees of the public will. Law, for Story, has a transcendent property that is impervious to superficial swings in public sentiment. He did not believe that democratic principles should be ignored; only that law should not be susceptible to changes that were only temporary, or reactive. "Laws are the very soul of a people; not merely those which are contained in the letter of their ordinances and statute books, but still more those which have grown up of themselves from their manners, and religion and history" (Story 1829–1833, 350). In the same text Story further pushes the point when he says that law is "founded, not upon any will, but on the discovery of a right already existing, which is to be drawn either from the internal legislation of human reason, or the historical development of a nation" (Story 1829–1833, 365). Story harks back to the original understanding of common law in these quotes; he interjects human reason and natural law understanding back into a theory of law. Story interjects principles that we saw abandoned by Wilson and other Federalists. McDowell summarizes Story's position on law and his place in the development of U.S. jurisprudence most aptly.

Story was, in sum, the last major defender of the original understanding of equity as transmitted from Aristotle to Blackstone. He saw equity not as a mere set of procedural remedies but as a system of jurisprudence, an auxiliary to the strict law, which aimed at an understanding of justice that transcended the fluctuating decrees of popular consent. More than any other man of his time, Story sought to recover and preserve the ethical and moral basis of the law. He attempted this recovery and preservation through the scientific elaboration of the vast tradition of the common law, of which equity was a part (McDowell 1982, 85).

Unfortunately for Story, the only way he saw to protect this form of law was to develop a new science of equity—unfortunate because he failed to see the link between codification and the destruction of the common law he sought to preserve. The only way he saw that there could be an exact science of equity was through written law, and written law is inimical to common law, which is what Story was trying to preserve. Story fell into a trap, it seems. He wanted to preserve equity so badly that he was willing to compromise it to preserve it. He recognized that he could only sell the concept of equity if it were bounded from becoming too expansive and allowing for too much judicial discretion. While recognizing the connection between natural law and the principles of equity, he also recognized the dangers of leaving too much authority in the hands of the courts. These factors combined to give him the motivation for creating a new science of equity. This science sought to develop a system of equity which respected its foundations while limiting the possibility of tyranny from the bench. His focus was on procedural reforms of equity pleading as well as substantive equity. His intention was to make these principles certain, so that they could be followed by practitioners of the law, and thus preserved. Ultimately, the effort of Story was in many ways self-defeating.

Story was not the only one who miscalculated the output of the system he supported. Jackson got a system of law which was more statutory centered, a system that had been adopted by many states as well. While Jackson feared nationalism, the movement that he oversaw spawned a movement toward nationalism, if only through uniform adoption and application of the law by the states. Also, it became unclear how destroying the common law system would help preserve democratic principles. Before Jackson and the codification movement, the influence of the people was felt directly by the legislature through elections, and in a more subtle manner, the will of the people was felt by the courts. By eliminating, or seeking to eliminate, many of the common law attributes within the judiciary, Jackson and the codification movement limited the people to express their will only through elections and only by representation by the legislature. The more statute oriented and restricted the judiciary becomes, the less it can represent the express needs of the community, which is one of the perceived benefits of a common law system.

By the time the debate reached Story and Jackson, the natural law foundation had been stripped from the common law. Natural law rested on the idea of a force greater than the state that could be relied upon as a guide for justice. It was law independent of the state. Common law too was independent of the state. Common law is understood to be something independent of law created by men; it is shaped by history, custom, and belief. While common law judges are agents of the state, they traditionally served as advocates of the community. Common law set up a system of laws and not of men. By taking away the natural law foundation, the debate turned into how much power the general government should have with respect to the state governments. There was also a debate over how law-making duties should be split between the legislature and the judiciary. These debates do share a common thread with common law debates. The central concern is with the government's authority and how best to manage it without compromising stability or liberty. The debate over local versus national government, and legislative versus judiciary, is a direct derivative of the common law debate.

Section I C.1: Jeremy Bentham

Jeremy Bentham was the philosophical force behind codification, a term which he originally coined. Bentham sought a system which would bring about more certainty, order, and objectivity to a system of law that he saw as unruly. He wanted a system of procedure which was more technical than natural, and a system of law making which was more legislature than judge. While his direct involvement was primarily in England, his efforts and reforms were not lost on the Americans. Charles Warren suggests that Jeremy Bentham was one of the primary reasons the American movement toward codification took off as it did (Warren 1911, 508). Men such as James Fennimore Cooper openly cited Bentham, and the critics of codification focused their objections on Bentham's philosophy. The magnitude of his influence is debatable; the fact that he was a source of philosophical reinforcement is not. Therefore, I will bypass an analysis of Bentham's relative influence, and move directly to Bentham's proposed reforms and the reasons for them.

One of the arguments made by common law advocates is that law should be representative of tradition and history; these principles were discarded by Bentham. He relied on logic rather than history and tradition, since it was only through logic that the greatest good could be achieved, and since the greatest happiness for the greatest number was his principal objective, it was through logic that law should be developed (Bentham 1977). He understood the common law system to be overly technical in its procedures, which he understood to be a sign of an underdeveloped system of law in which principles of law are subordinate to procedure (Judson 1910, 48). Procedure in the courts was originally designed to bring about an alternative to violence as a way of dispute resolution. Therefore it was Bentham's understanding that after this initial stage of development, the system should move beyond a strict adherence to procedure toward a strict adherence to law. Bentham's ideas were expressed by former Supreme Court Chief Justice and President William H. Taft in his speech "Delays and Defects of the Enforcement of Law in the United States":

> If one were asked in what respect we had fallen farthest short of ideal conditions in our whole government, I think we would be justified in answering, in spite of the glaring defects of our system of municipal government, that it is in our failure to secure expedition and thoroughness in the enforcement of public and private rights in our courts. (Taft 1969)

Taft goes on to attribute this failure to the glacial pace at which things move through the courts and the high costs of seeking resolution through the court system.

Bentham did not concern himself solely with procedure, but opposed common law on the grounds that it was judge-made law. Instead he supported a system of legislature-made law. He sought the substitution of unwritten with written law based on the philosophic principles that would bring about the greatest happiness for mankind (Bentham 1977). He argued that the courts were only in place to resolve disputes surrounding laws that were established by the legislature, thus placing the burden on the legislature to come up with a wholly comprehensive system of law. He, like Andrew Jackson, saw the legislature as the only branch that was capable of having the interests of the many at heart when they made decisions. Thus, law making was best placed in their hands. He deduced his ideas for legislative dominance from his greatest happiness principle. Bentham created a number of policies to be adopted by the legislature that would bring about the greatest happiness. Bentham wanted to bring about reform through the legislature since the court system was typically slow to respond, making rapid reforms difficult to implement.

Things done through the courts are typically done incrementally, but through the legislature sweeping reforms can be made, given the proper majority. It was his belief in drastic reform and rapid change that led to his opposition to the English court system, and by extension the American. The reliance on history, tradition, and precedent were impediments to Bentham's proposed reforms.[6] For Bentham, the only way to bring about his reforms was by sweeping aside the common law system so that the legislature could quickly enact policies that would achieve the greatest happiness principle. It was through codification that the greatest happiness principle could be achieved, since the courts relied too much on procedure, history, and precedent. The courts, as they were in Bentham's time, were a hindrance and an archaic system that could not bring about the greatest happiness principle which could be achieved through codification. This line of reasoning was not without its critics; Blackstone offers a lengthy critique of codification.

When laws are to be framed by popular assemblies, even of the representative kind, it is too Herculean a task to begin the work of legislation afresh, and extract a new system from the discordant opinions of more than five hundred counselors. A single legislator or an enterprising sovereign, a Solon or Lycurgus, a Justinian or a Frederick, may at any time form a concise, and perhaps a uniform, plan of justice; and evil betide that presumptuous subject who questions its wisdoms or utility. But who, acquainted with the difficulty of new-modeling any branch of our statute laws (though relating but to roads or to parish settlements), will conceive it ever feasible to alter any fundamental point of the common law, with all it appendages and consequents, and set up another rule in its stead? (Blackstone 1979, 267)

Bentham was little concerned with the social order, only the problems of welfare and utility. This led him to the idea that institutions and human nature were easily mutable only if the correct policies were enacted. He did not consider that individuals had an attachment to the old way of things, and that such rapid change might have created a disruption that he did not account for. Furthermore, Bentham's reliance on the legislature leads to the same conclusions, with respect to majority rule, as Jackson's reliance on the legislature did. Bentham is a positivist, and he considers that the only valid laws are those promulgated or passed by some government entity. He ignores the validity of natural law and common law with this position.

Section I D: What This All Means

Tracing the path from the ratification debates to Bentham shows that the development of American jurisprudence has centered on a common theme. The theme is whether the law should be in the hands of formal government institutions or be left under the control of a more ambiguous system. Those seeking to move the power to formal institutions seek more certainty and a clearer definition of the law. Conversely, those seeking the less formal system argue that justice is better served under a flexible system that is responsive to the needs of the community, though entrenched enough not to be swayed by every shift of the public will. The formal institution proponents seek a system which provides a definitive outcome while the other side favors a system in which the outcomes are representative. A statute-oriented system in favor of positive law over natural law is the system favored by the first group. Common law is a system of law which carries with it the same principles argued for by the second group I have described.

While the debates in each era that I covered did not focus solely on the common law, they did take into account various common law principles. The conclusion that can be drawn from this brief history is that common law has been compromised and it is the result of seeking to bring more certainty and control to the law. The standard method of reining in law has been through codification. Codified laws are theoretically antithetical to common law, and in practice the gradual codification of laws undertaken at the state and national level has directly led to a compromise of common law.

The empirical analysis focuses on those areas of modern jurisprudence that were previously a part of common law jurisdiction and have successfully been taken out of that system through codification. These four areas include crime, commerce, sentencing, and procedure. The final section will analyze the development of the principal attribute of the common law system: the jury. An empirical analysis will provide sound evidence for establishing what factors contribute to the abandonment of common law, whether it is the desire for certainty or some other variables.

SECTION II: RESEARCH DESIGN

Section II A: Uniform Commercial Code

From medieval Europe through the American colonial period, commerce fell under common law jurisdiction. Disputes over land and water usage were settled by local barristers in the presence of a jury. When disputes arose between purchaser and merchant it was "buyer beware," but if that policy failed, the case was heard in a local court. But as the states began to experience economic growth, they also experienced increased complications with that growth. Furthermore, as commerce increased, so too did the chance for disputes to arise. Beginning in the late eighteenth and early nineteenth centuries, there was a shift in the way commercial disputes arose and were dealt with. Part of the shift is attributed to the changing individual:

> It was also becoming apparent that the ideal man was no longer an essentially spiritual being who devoted himself to the pursuit of religious ends; he was coming instead to be viewed as an essentially economic being who devoted himself to the pursuit of material ends. (Nelson 1994, 154)

In addition to the changing character of the individual, cases were being dealt with differently in the courts. These changes were in part affected by the changing legislation that was passed at both the state and national level in response to pressures by both creditors and debtors. "They sought and obtained legislation that increased their remedies against the real estate of deceased debtors, remedies that became increasingly valuable as the land market matured" (Nelson 1994, 151).

It was not only legislation and disputes in relation to deceased land holders. Water usage became more complicated with mechanization and interstate commerce. It became increasingly difficult to settle matters that occurred in a particular jurisdiction when the owners of the company were separate from the operators, and the operators lived outside of that jurisdiction. If a paper mill in Pennsylvania was accused of unnecessarily damming a stream for its use, and the owner lived in New York, common law courts had difficulty exercising jurisdiction. Moreover, if that dispute was raised by another company whose owner resided in Connecticut, it likely became a matter for the federal court system.

Commerce is a prime dependent variable since it was an area that was previously under common law jurisdiction and then shifted outside of that jurisdiction due to legislative and environmental changes. I have chosen the Uniform Commercial Code (UCC) as the dependent variable which measures changes in commerce. That is, when a state adopts the UCC it is taken to mean, in this study, that commerce is no longer a common law matter in that state. The National Conference of Commissioners on Uniform State Laws (NCUSL) was created in 1892 on the recommendation and encouragement of the American Bar Association (ABA). The mission of the NCUSL was to create uniformity in the state laws. The NCUSL is staffed by lawyers chosen from the states to prepare laws that are proposed to the states for their individual adoption.[7] One of the sets of laws to come out of this process was the UCC in 1952. The UCC was passed at the national level in 1952, and given to each of the state legislatures to adopt at their own pace, and by 1967 all states except Louisiana had adopted at least some part of the UCC.

The UCC will be constructed in two different ways so that it will serve as the dependent variable for two different models. In both models, the analysis will be done using an event history analysis, also known as a duration model. Since the states could adopt the UCC on their own pace, an event history analysis will be used by coding the UCC adoption period for each state as duration data. This will allow an investigation into why some states took longer to adopt than others. The first model will use the UCC to measure the Initial Adoption by the states. Since the UCC could be adopted in parts, and was not required to be adopted as a whole, the initial adoption time varied across states. But to capture when the entire UCC was adopted, the dependent variable Total Adoption will be used in order to understand what factors contributed to the initial and complete adoption, and whether different variables affected the adoption decision in different ways.

To test the hypothesis that the speed and degree of UCC adoption is a result of a state's increasing incompatibility with common law principles will require the inclusion of a number of independent variables, some of which it is appropriate to describe here. First, the adoption time for the UCC may be modeled as a consequence of the state's legislature; a full-time, professional legislature is more likely to adopt new codes more quickly than a state like Texas which has a part-time legislature. Second, to test Nelson's claim that increasing complexity in commerce leads to increased legislation, the state's gross domestic product (GDP) will be included for each year. An increasing GDP is taken to mean an increased complexity in that state's commercial system. In conjunction with a state's GDP to discern the level of commercial complexity will be a measure for urbanization, the amount of that state's population which resides in cities. Third, as the ABA was an official proponent of uniformity in state laws, the amount of ABA involvement in each state as measured by the number of members of the bar in that state is an additional variable. Finally, it should be noted that this is not a comprehensive list of the explanatory variables, which is reserved for chapter 3 when the empirical analysis will be performed.

Section II B: Sentencing Guidelines

At the beginning of this project I outlined a number of characteristics intrinsic to a common law system, and one of those is a jury's ability, under the observance of the judge, to decide the sentence for the defendant if found guilty. Sentencing guidelines take this right away from the courts, and place it into the hands of the legislatures and sentencing commissions. The Federal Sentencing Commission, whose current guidelines are in place, was created in 1984. This commission created guidelines for the federal government while creating a model for the states to follow. The first dependent variable which will be used here is the state adoption of sentencing guidelines through a sentencing commission established in that state. Since no state with a sentencing commission has failed to implement that state's policies, I will use the date the commission was created instead of when the policy was adopted. This serves several purposes: (1) it allows investigation independent of legislative characteristics, (2) the legislature is not completely ignored since legislative action is required to fund a commission, and (3) the length of time between commission creation and law enactment depends on variables which are of little interest to a study on common law. This variable is the duration between the establishment of the Federal Sentencing Commission and each state's sentencing commission. The observation period begins in 1984 and ends in 2002 with the establishment of the last state commission, in South Carolina. This will be an event history analysis.

Nearly all states have some sort of legislative passed guidelines in place to limit judicial discretion, but legislative originated and passed policies are not necessarily violations of democratic principles, and democratic principles such as accountability and representation are principles shared with common law. The problem and the violation of common law principles lies in the unelected commissions that establish these guidelines independent of voter involvement. These commissions create guidelines independent of any representative feature or mechanism for accountability. And for the most part the guidelines handed down from the federal government are adopted by these commissions. Under the common law system the sentencing was left in the local courts since it was the courts that had some sense of the needs and values of the community. With sentencing guidelines a national commission hands down guidelines to a state commission, and neither commission is required to take into account the needs and values of the community. Although these guidelines must be voted on by the state's legislature before they are enacted, there is generally limited opposition to the guidelines handed down by the commissions. In fact, no commission recommendation has been rejected when given a vote in the legislature.

Some of the independent variables will be shared with the UCC analysis, but some new ones, unique to sentencing, will be used. First, crime rates are expected to lead to the creation of sentencing commissions. As crime rates increase there is typically pressure for politicians to take action, and that action is to get "tough on crime," while public perception may be different from reality, and there may at times be public outcry to do something about crime even when the crime rate is relatively mild. These occasions are not of concern here. The way that this study has been set up is to show that revisions to, and limitations of, common law jurisdiction take place by government officials who seek to create a solution to a problem through legislation rather than allowing the problem to be settled through common law channels where it had previously resided.

Section II C: Civil Procedure Reform

These reforms come about in the same way that the above reforms do. There is a federal commission which develops a model that is implemented at the national level. The states then typically establish commissions to adopt the national model and shape it to their specific needs and give it to the state legislature to be voted on and enacted. The method of adopting civil procedure reform is no different, and since it follows a similar pattern of adoption as both the UCC and sentencing, it will be analyzed in the same way, through an event history analysis. The relevance of the variable may not be as clear as sentencing, but it is not to be discounted because its relevancy is not obvious.

The variables on the right-hand side of the equation will be those that were used in the UCC and sentencing guidelines. The advocates of a uniform system in the previous two areas were the same as those who wanted civil procedure reform. The particular variables of interest will be ABA involvement, number of trial judges in the state, and various measures for societal complexity. I will include one additional variable, that of English heritage; those states that were previously governed by the English will have a stronger attachment to the common law system of pleading, and should therefore adopt the reforms at a later date due to their increased resistance.

Section II D: Common Law Crime

In nearly all states, their original constitution contained a phrase that said something to the effect that all common law crimes that do not conflict with the crimes as defined by the constitution or future legislation will remain in effect. There are some states that through legislation invalidated common law crimes, and established that only those crimes defined by statute or constitution will be recognized as crimes in that state. This violates the principles of common law in at least three ways.[8] First, common law is explicitly invalidated as a source of defining crime. Second, these statutes mean that crimes that were previously crimes only because of precedent are no longer crimes. This is essentially saying that precedent is invalid when making decisions on crime. Third, crimes are not defined in the community in a manner that serves the community's best interest but instead are homogenized to serve the general welfare of the state. While this may be desirable, it is not the objective of common law.

This again will be an event history analysis. The first year of the duration will be the first year a state abolished a common law crime, 1923, and the investigation period ends in the final year a state abolished common law crime,

1989. The hypothesis is that common law crime is replaced by statutory crime in order to bring more stability to the system. Crime rate will again be used. An increase in crime rate may be attributed to the varying definitions of crime, and a uniform system established through legislation will eliminate this variation and lead to a decrease in crime.

Section II E: The Jury System

From 1976 to 2002, twenty-three states have tracked and reported what proportion of their trials were heard by a jury as opposed to a bench trial. This is relevant information to a study on the common law since a jury is one of the hallmarks of a common law system. This information will be used as a time-series analysis showing what factors lead to an increased or decreased use of jury trials. Two independent variables which are expected to have an impact on the percentage of jury trials are urbanization and crime rate. As the total number of people increases so too will the number of trials, and the same is true for crime rate; as the crime rate increases so will docket size. The accepted understanding of common law is that it exists in a non-litigious community whose population is somewhat small and less economically complex. Therefore, the three independent variables I include capture both these effects and satisfactorily test the hypothesis: urbanization, population growth, and industrialization.

NOTES

1. See also *Federalist Papers* 55 and 72.
2. All references to *The Federalist Papers* are to the Carey and McClellan (2001) edition.
3. It has already been concluded that Wilson's position is contrary to common law principles as he takes away natural law and man's ability to know right from wrong across all cases.
4. While jury trials are guaranteed by the Constitution at the district level, at the appellate level there is no such assurance. Secondly, the jury must be of the defendant's peers, and given the enlarged geographical boundaries of the federal district, it is unlikely that the jury will be chosen entirely from the defendant's community.
5. More traditional proponents of common law see it as an all or nothing system. Common law can work alongside statutory law, but statutory law and codification cannot infringe on common law jurisdiction without violating its most basic principles.
6. Bentham's position was almost the opposite of William Blackstone, who supported a system of law which was grounded in the history and traditions of the

community, and who considered procedure to be as much a part of the law as anything else.

7. The commission also seeks the guidance of law professionals, lawyers and academics who specialize in a particular field.

8. It has been pointed out that statute law is not completely independent of common law, but in the way that I define common law crime and statute crime the two are at odds. For instance, prior to the 1950s it was understood in Connecticut that alcohol was not to be sold on Sundays; it was a common law. When the state no longer allowed for crimes to be defined by any other means than through statute or constitution, stores began selling alcohol on Sundays, leading to public backlash and forcing the legislature to make a statute banning the sale of alcohol on Sundays. This is typical of what are known as "Blue Laws" that impose restrictions on what retail stores can do on Sundays; many of these "Blue Laws" have lost much of their force.

3

An Evaluation of the Factors that Have Led to the Dismantling

The study of policy innovation and diffusion at the state level is not necessarily a new area of study, although the policies that this manuscript focus on have not been analyzed in this manner before. The bulk of policy diffusion literature has tended to focus on topics such as education reform (Mintrom and Vergari 1998), welfare programs (Barrilleaux, Holbrook, and Langer 2002), and patterns of lottery adoption (Berry and Berry 1990). By performing a comparative state-level analysis the researcher is able to approach a level of control generally found only in experiments. In order to draw reliable conclusions about the impact of a variable, the researcher must be able to successfully isolate the impact of that variable by controlling other factors which might lead to variation in the dependent variable (Campbell and Stanley 1966; King, Keohane, and Verba 1994). This sort of control can be successfully accomplished in state-level analysis since the states share a number of common characteristics that are naturally controlled for, making it easier to isolate those variables which are of interest to the researcher. This study will include variables that are intended to measure institutional, political, and societal variations across the states.[1] It is hypothesized that institutions and society interact in such a way that the changes in society create an opportunity for government officials to make institutional changes at the urging of interest groups, but the institutional changes that are made limit the amount of community involvement that can take place in the future in that particular area by putting the power to make such changes in the hands of the government.[2] Using an event history approach allows for a natural integration of time which means some conclusions can be drawn about the historical development of these policies as well.

In 1969 Jack Walker wrote *The Diffusion of Innovations among the American States*, which opened the door to political science research on policy innovation and diffusion. Walker studied external factors on the budgetary process in order to correct for previous research that he felt provided inadequate explanations of public policy outcomes. He wanted "to develop propositions which might be used as guides to the study of the diffusion of innovations" (Walker 1969, 881). He investigates the speed of innovation adoption and discerns what patterns develop. Walker focuses his attention on the diffusion patterns of innovations. He runs a factor analysis and finds that external determinants strongly impact the pattern of diffusion and speed of adoption. Walker finds that states like New York and California act as policy leaders and states tend to emulate programs adopted in these two states. But more often than relying on California and New York, policymakers look to states within their region for the innovation of ideas.

One of the first works to employ Walker's strategy was Virginia Gray's (1973). Gray creates a model of the diffusion process for education, welfare, and civil rights. She finds that the patterns of diffusion vary within the various innovations of welfare and civil rights programs, while in education, most innovations follow a similar pattern. Although she agrees with Walker's internal determinants of initial adopting states, she contends that policy diffusion patterns depend on the policy area and the degree of federal involvement.

Falling in line with Walker (1969) and Gray (1973), Welch and Thompson (1980) investigate the impact of federal incentives on policy diffusion. They look at both positive and negative federal incentives in the policy areas of education, health, welfare, agriculture, civil rights, and the environment. The authors find that the federal incentives, whether positive or negative, "greatly speed the rate of policy diffusion through the states" (Welch and Thompson 1980, 723). However, a positive incentive will diffuse faster than a negative one. They take Gray to task when they conclude that the specific policy area has only a minor impact on the diffusion rate.

Canon and Baum (1981) examine the internal determinants in the diffusion of judicial innovations. They study the rate of state adoption of twenty-three tort law doctrines from 1876 to 1975. Using a similar formula to Walker's, they compute a composite innovation score. With judicial innovations, they find that internal determinants characterize the states with higher adoption rates. However, they find "little evidence of regionalism in the diffusion of tort doctrines" (Canon and Baum 1981, 985), countering Walker's initial findings.

In examining the research of policy innovation and diffusion, Berry and Berry (1990) find that the internal and external factors of policy innovation and diffusion were usually separated in the analysis. They argue that "neither a pure regional model nor a pure internal determinants model is a plausible explanation of state innovation in isolation" (Berry and Berry 1990, 396). This separate treatment leads to inaccurate explanations of state policy innovation and diffusion. Berry and Berry believe a combined model that encompasses both of these internal and external explanations should be used in state policy innovation and diffusion studies. On the basis of an event history analysis model, they find that internal determinants like a state's economic situation and election year, along with external factors like regionalism, have a major impact on the probability of a state's adoption of a lottery.

Other researchers have applied Berry and Berry's integrated model of diffusion to different areas of public policy. Mooney and Lee (1995; 1999) examine whether diffusion patterns are similar with regard to morality politics of abortion and the death penalty. Michael Mintrom (1997; 2000) studies the impact of policy entrepreneurs on the diffusion of school choice reforms. Each of these studies builds upon the methodological foundation laid by Berry and Berry. The research of Berry and Berry has been important not just because of their substantive findings, but the methodological impact it has had on the field as well. The application of an event history analysis has now become common among researchers studying state policy diffusion and adoption patterns, and it is the strategy I will use in this chapter.

SECTION I: EVENT HISTORY ANALYSIS

The statistical analysis in chapter 3 will be carried out using an event history analysis (EHA).[3] This method of analysis has been used quite extensively by those interested in policy adoption patterns among the states as well as those in international relations interested in the duration of alliances and wars. With EHA the researcher begins with a risk set, the risk set; contains those entities (that is, states) which are at risk for experiencing the event (that is, policy adoption). For every year in the study a zero is entered for the event except for the year the policy is adopted, when a one is entered. The goal of EHA is to explain what factors contribute to the occurrence of an event, and at what rate. The duration, or length of time, it takes for the event to occur is reflected in the hazard rate.[4] The hazard rate is the likelihood of an event; a decreasing hazard indicates a longer duration, and an increasing hazard indicates a decreasing duration.

There is one primary advantage for using EHA over ordinary least squares (OLS). Event history models allow the researcher to include censored and truncated data; these are data which do not occur within the specified time frame either because they occurred before the study began, or the study ends before the event occurred for a particular unit. "The use of OLS regression on data which take the form of some finite length of time is inappropriate. Since duration data are strictly positive, the assumption of normally distributed errors made by OLS regression is violated" (Bennett and Stam 1996). With OLS, states that adopted prior to this study's sample would be omitted, and states that adopted after this study's sample would be treated as if they adopted in 2002; EHA remedies both of these problems.

There are a number of duration models available to researchers; the most common in political science are the Cox Proportional Hazard Model and the Weibull Model. The Weibull model assumes that the baseline hazard model is either monotonically decreasing or increasing, whereas the Cox model allows the researcher to leave the baseline hazard unparameterized.

For this reason, the Cox model is sometimes referred to as a "semi-parametric" model: the (ordered) duration times are parameterized in terms of a set of covariates, but the particular distributional form of the duration times is not parameterized (Box-Steffensmeier and Jones 2004, 49).

Unless the researcher has a strong enough theory to suggest that the baseline hazard is constant, increasing, or decreasing, leaving the baseline unparameterized makes sense. A researcher can always test his data and then go back and choose the model, but this would seem to invite the same criticisms one gets from using step-wise regression (King 1986). Since my theory does not lead me to conclude anything about the shape of the baseline hazard function I will leave it unparameterized and use the Cox model for each of the policies I study.

SECTION II: POLICIES AND VARIABLES

This chapter focuses on several different policies, all of which will be treated separately within the chapter. The inclusion of so many different policies serves a specific purpose—common law is complex, and no single variable can capture it entirely. As was explained in chapters 1 and 2, there are many facets to common law, which makes the incorporation of so many policies necessary to adequately capture the effect. Each policy will include are different specification, but they will also share some variables, and it is these shared variables that will allow for a triangulation of sorts. That is to say, if these policies each represent a facet of common law, and a specific variable reacts the same way for each policy, then it will be concluded that the variable acts that way in relation to common law as a whole.

Section II A: Dependent Variables 1 and 2

The Uniform Commercial Code (UCC) is a code developed at the national level, and recommended to the states for adoption. The primary intention of the UCC was to bring a level of uniformity to commerce among the states that had not previously existed. States did not have to adopt the entire set of codes, and instead had the option of selecting which parts they felt were appropriate for them.[5] Therefore, it will be useful to use two separate models to study the UCC, Initial UCC and Total UCC. An EHA will be performed once with the event being the initial adoption in that state, and again with the event being the total adoption of the UCC. Obviously for those states that did not initially adopt the UCC in its entirety, Total UCC will occur later than Initial UCC.

Section II A.1: Independent Variables

ABA: This variable measures the involvement of the American Bar Association within a state by calculating the number of attorneys in that state per one thousand people. It is important to use a ratio and not a raw count since the influence of a group increases as a function of its size relative to the rest of the population. Given the history laid out in chapter 2, and the role that the ABA played in pushing for uniform codes in a number of areas, it seems reasonable to hypothesize that the more concentrated the lawyer population, the more quickly a state will adopt a uniform code (Source: *The Lawyer Statistical Report: The U.S. Legal Profession*).

Party Competition: I have derived this variable from the Ranney Index. The Ranney Index uses party control in state institutions to derive the level of party competition within the state. The values given when computed range from 0 to 1. A score from 0 to .250 means a state is Republican controlled and from 1 to .750 indicates control by the Democratic Party. The scale can be further broken down to show whether the state leans in one direction or whether there is perfect competition.[6] I adopt these scores, along with the conventional breakdown, and "fold" the scores.(Ranney 1976; Bibby and Holbrook 2004). A state that has perfect or near perfect competition receives a score of 3, a state that leans in a direction gets a 2, and one-party dominated states are coded 1.[7] It is anticipated that the more competitive the party structure, the shorter the duration until policy adoption. Or to put it the other way, a state with a one-party dominant system is likely to see a longer duration. This is because the policies I have chosen are to some degree neutral; they do not seem to benefit either party's traditional agenda. Thus, as hypothesized by E. E. Schattschneider, an equally balanced system is more likely to pass neutral legislation whereas a one-party dominant system will produce partisan legislation (Schattschneider 1960, Source: *Book of the States* and author's calculations).

Growth: This variable measures the change of growth in the state government by measuring the number of people the government employs from year to year; this variable measures the percentage of growth in government employment levels compared to the previous year. This measure is adopted from Weiher and Lorence (1991). Thus we would expect to see a shorter duration for those states that have high levels of growth. The hypothesis that this variable is intended to measure was developed by William E. Nelson (1994). Nelson (1994) states that increasing government size will lead to a shift away from the common law. The greater the change of growth in the state government, the more quickly a state is expected to adopt a policy that amends the common law. Thus we would expect to see a shorter duration for those states that have a high percentage of growth (*Book of the States*).

State GDP: A state's gross domestic product is intended to complement the Growth variable, and is motivated by the same theoretical concept, which is, as the complexity of a society increases, the more likely the decline in common law. For State GDP, the argument is that, as the complexity of a state's commercial system increases, the more likely it is to adopt rules to regulate commerce through uniformity. The hypothesis that leads to the inclusion of this variable was also developed by William Nelson (1994). In addition to being concerned with government growth, Nelson says that the increasing complexity of society caused a shift away from traditional common law in Massachusetts (*Book of the States*).

Bills Passed: Legislatures which pass a high number of bills per year are more likely to adopt a uniform code than are those states with legislatures that pass fewer bills, and therefore act more slowly. States are broken into five categories with 5 being the most active, and 1 the least. For example, Alaska falls into category 1 with around 250 bills passed per year, and California is in category 5 passing an average near two thousand a year (*Book of the States*).

Full-Time Legislature: This is a dummy variable coded 1 for states with a full-time legislature and 0 for states with a part-time legislature. The logic for this variable is the same as the one above. A full-time legislature is apt to be quicker to adopt new policies since it meets more regularly (*Book of the States*).

Section II B: Dependent Variable 3

Initially, most states recognized common law crime in their constitutions. Chapter 1 makes this point by saying that common law serves as a legitimizing force to a new regime since the common law is a system that is steeped in tradition and history, a history and tradition that is shared in common by the population which is governed by the new constitution. A new regime has no codified laws except those in its constitution, and the first session of its legislature is unlikely to create a comprehensive set of laws, instead choosing to focus on those matters that are most pressing. So simply as a matter of convenience common law receives initial support in a state's constitution. Some states, after a period of time passes, tend to pass legislation or adopt constitutional amendments which nullify common law crimes and then instruct their court to recognize only those crimes addressed by constitution or statute.

In creating the model for common law crime I use many of the same variables from the UCC model: ABA, State GDP, Growth, Party Competition, Full-Time Legislature, and Bills Passed.[8] The variables listed below are used for common law crime and not the UCC.

Section II B.1: Independent Variables

State Population: The logic for including this variable is similar to some of the others. As state population grows, matters such at crime presumably become more difficult to manage within a common law system. Therefore, a state which has a large population will tend toward codification more quickly than one that has a smaller population (*Book of the States*).

Particularity of State Constitution: This measure is adopted from the work of Christopher Hammons (1999). This measure is a percentage of the particularistic content within a state constitution. A constitution with more particularistic content will presumably be inclined to a more rigid, or at least codified, system of law, something different from the common law system. Therefore, a state with a high level of particularistic content will abandon common law crime more quickly than a state that does not have such a high level of particularistic content (Hammons 1999).

Section II C: Dependent Variable 4

In a common law system the judge has the power of sentencing the convicted once a jury has made the determination of guilt. In some instances juries make the decisions on sentencing within parameters set by the presiding judge. The current Federal Guidelines were established in 1984, but just as the UCC was spurred on by the NCUSL, so too was a move toward uniform sentencing guidelines. This system of establishing sentencing guidelines outside of the courtroom, by a commission which is separate from the particularities of the case whose guidelines it will impact, takes away one of the key features of a common law system. The purpose of giving sentencing discretion directly to judges is to ensure that the community's interest is served. In England the common law judge was used as an agent of the Crown to make decisions at the local level. While judges had to stay committed to the Crown, they were given some leeway in how they enforced the laws. The judge was closer to the community than the Crown and in the common law setting, thereby tying the judge to the community in some respects. On some occasions the judge would hand down guidelines to the jury and let the jury make the final decision; by turning over the final decision to the jury, the sentence would mirror the sentiment of the community even more. By establishing guidelines at a centralized level, discretion is taken out of the hands of judge and jury, thereby increasing the risk that sentences will violate the community's sense of justice.

Three variables, ABA, State GDP and Full-Time Legislature, are used in this model with the same anticipated results as in the UCC and Common Law Crime models. Four new variables are added to this model as they are not applicable to the above models.

Section II C.1: Independent Variables

Percent Urban: This measures the percentage of the state's population that resides in urban areas. While it could be used for the UCC and Common Law Crime, there is a high rate of multicollinearity between this variable and the Growth variable which is included in the other two models. A state with a high rate of urbanization will tend toward a system of certainty more quickly than one that does not, due to the increased complexity that comes with large urban centers, as well as the increased workload urban courts experience. Time spent on sentencing is time that can be spent on other areas. Support for a sentencing commission that will establish guidelines to help alleviate some of the time constraints on judges will be supported in areas with a high percentage of urbanization (*Book of the States*).

Number of Judges: This variable serves as a complement to ABA since the judges in each state are drawn from the Bar. Therefore, as the number of judges increases so too will the hazard rate, meaning the time to failure will decrease. A sentencing commission takes some of the authority away from the judges, but the workload for the judges also diminishes since they do not have to spend as much time on sentencing since guidelines have already been set. Judges are continually looking for ways to effectively manage their workloads; it seems reasonable that they would be in support of sentencing guidelines. Sentencing commissions are staffed by a combination of legal experts, judges, and attorneys, so judges are not releasing as much authority as it may seem at first glance. Since there is no evidence of multicollinearity when both

Number of Judges and ABA are used in the model, there is a benefit to including both (*Book of the States*).

Judge Selection Method: The method of selecting judges varies per state, and which method is used means that the selection process is influenced by different forces. Judge Selection Method ranks the selection methods by level of influence by that state's Bar.[9] The hazard rate would be expected to increase as the system in place favors the Bar. For a system like Texas in which every judge is elected, thus Bar influence minimized, one would expect there to be a longer duration than in a state like Virginia, which appoints the majority of their judges (*Book of the States*).[10]

Section II D: Dependent Variable 5

In 1938 the same forces that brought about the UCC and other uniform laws created a method of civil procedure which would expedite the process by regulating such things as discovery and method of pleading. This reform eliminated many of the features of the original common law system of pleading. In one sense, the adoption of this reform is a direct assault on the common law system by further integrating systems of law and equity into a single system, a movement which began in the mid-1800s with the Codification Movement that was discussed in chapter 2. All of the variables, except for one, used in this model have been discussed above: ABA, Party Competition, Growth, State Population, Bills Passed, and Full-Time Legislature. All of these variables are expected to act in the ways hypothesized above as well, and for similar reasons, since the dependent variable in question is still a proxy for common law.

Section II D.1: Independent Variables

Industrial: The level of industrialization in a state is predicted to act in much the same way as State GDP and Percent Urban. While State GDP and Industrialization are intended to measure a similar phenomenon, State GDP and State Population are linearly related and therefore cannot be used in the model. Industrialization is linearly related with State Population, but the relation is not as strong with State GDP and can still be used in conjunction with Industrial without significantly increasing the amount of variance (*Book of the States*).

SECTION III: AND THE RESULTS ARE IN

After looking at all the models, one feels quite comfortable drawing conclusions with respect to the role each variable plays in the state's decision to adopt the various policies in question. The idea behind using different models was to triangulate the effect these variables had on common law development within the states. There is no single policy that can be used as an adequate proxy for common law; therefore, using four[11] policies that represent a different aspect of common law is useful and will lead to more convincing results. But in order to draw a conclusion regarding the impact of the variables selected, the variables which are shared across the models must impact the adoption decision in a similar way. Little could be concluded if a variable had a negative impact in one model, a positive impact in another, and no impact in a third model.

There are seven variables that are shared by at least four models, and two variables that are shared by all five of the models, and the shared variables each act in the same direction across the models. For instance, ABA, the variable which measures the involvement of the state's Bar, has an increasing hazard ratio in all of the models. This means that when the ABA is involved the duration before policy adoption is shortened, a finding which supports my hypothesis. For purposes of clarity I will report the findings for each policy, and then discuss the policies together in the concluding section. Since the Uniform Commercial Code uses two different duration models, I will discuss the two models together under the same heading.

Section III A: Uniform Commercial Code

Both models, Initial UCC and Total UCC, were identically specified. Each contains the same six variables. The most surprising result in each of the models came from the Growth variable—it acted opposite of the anticipated direction. I had expected, as theory directed, that increasing Growth would lead to a more rapid adoption of uniform policies, when in fact it appears to have the opposite effect. Since existing theory does not anticipate this, the only explanation I can give is an alternative hypothesis whose only backing is found in these data. Perhaps states with a high level of government growth are states which are not susceptible to change brought on by outside forces. States that employ a large number of people would necessarily be resistant to change since the livelihood of a larger percentage of the population is at stake. Furthermore, growth says something about strength. A state which shows signs of growth might also be a state which is able to resist outside pressure to change. While the data I have compiled cannot be used to test these hypotheses, perhaps they can be adequately tested in another study. Despite the unanticipated results from Growth, there are variables in each of the models that reach statistical significance and act in the anticipated direction. I will deal with the Initial UCC model first.

As seen in table 3.1, both ABA, Party Competition, State GDP, and Full-Time Legislature act as anticipated, and reach statistical significance. Each has an increasing hazard ratio, which means a shorter duration before policy adoption. So in accordance with my hypothesis, a state with a strong contingency of attorneys, and thus Bar, will adopt a uniform code more quickly than a state that is not as strongly influenced by the state Bar. So we can say that states with high levels of party competition initially adopted the UCC more quickly. Used as a measure for complexity, State GDP signals that the more complex commercial matters become, the more quickly the government will act to bring about a level of uniformity. Lastly, Full-Time Legislature acts as anticipated, which is to say, a legislature which is professional and in session year-round will adopt policies more quickly than a state which has a part-time legislature which only meets for a few months every other year.

Table 3.2 shows the results from the Cox Proportional Hazard Model when the Total UCC is considered. As stated earlier, this model uses the time in which the state had completely adopted the UCC as its failure point. Just as in the Initial UCC model, the ABA, Party Competition, and Full-Time Legislature variables act in the anticipated direction. An additional variable, Bills Passed, is statistically significant and acts in the anticipated direction. This variable indicates that the more active a state's legislature is the more quickly they will adopt a new policy. According to tables 3.1 and 3.2 we see that Full-Time active state legislatures act quickly to adopt new policies. Based on table 3.1 Growth acts as we should expect, but the findings in table 3.2 for State GDP are surprising.

Table 3.1. Factors that Influence the Initial Adoption of the Uniform Commercial Code

Variables	*Hazard Ratio*[1] *(Standard Error)*	*Percentage Change in Hazard Rate*
ABA	1.001* (.0009)	.1
Growth	.981* (.0064)	−1.9
State GDP	1.002* (.0007)	.2
Full-Time Legislature	1.556* (.5016)	55.6
Bills Passed	1.026* (.1303)	2.6
Party Competition	1.448* (.3261)	44.8

N = 2150 Log-Likelihood = −123.22 Chi-Square = 50.51
*Significant with One-Tailed T-Test at < .05
[1]A hazard ratio less than 1 means that it is decreasing and greater than 1 means that it is increasing.

Table 3.2. Factors Influencing Total Adoption of the Uniform Commercial Code

Variables	*Hazard Ratio (Standard Error)*	*Percentage Change in Hazard Rate*
ABA	1.002* (.0009)	.2
Growth	.981* (.0057)	−1.9
State GDP	.999* (.0003)	−.2
Full-Time Legislature	1.343* (.4615)	34.3
Bills Passed	.735* (.1100)	−26.5
Party Competition	1.700* (.4172)	70

N = 2150 Log-Likelihood = −136.92 Chi-Square = 23.10
*Significant with One-Tailed T-Test at < .05

The findings in table 3.2 seem to suggest that the higher the State GDP, the longer it will take that state to adopt a new uniform policy. Perhaps State GDP and Growth somehow represent government strength, and a strong state government is more likely to resist influence from outside forces, even if that outside force is the national government. Or, State GDP and Growth may be signs of prosperity, and a state which is enjoying a time of prosperity may not want to "upset the apple cart" by adopting new policies that may alter the system. This is a reasonable assumption from the standpoint of both variables, but particularly the State GDP since the UCC deals directly with commerce, something that has a direct bearing on GDP. But since the data I have compiled are unable to test these new hypotheses I will leave them to future research. But since State GDP acts opposite in tables 3.1 and 3.2, any conclusions concerning this variable should be tentative.

From both tables we see that there is, it seems, a substantively small effect of ABA on the hazard rate. A percentage change of 0.1 means that for a one-unit change in value of ABA there is a percent change in the hazard rate of 0.1.[12] ABA is measured as the number of attorneys per one thousand population, so every time there is an attorney added and the population stays the same, the hazard rate increases by less than 1 percent. This point is reinforced by the findings in table 3.2. The reader needs to keep in mind when examining these results, that there has been a rapid increase in the number of attorneys over the past forty years, an increase which far outpaces the population growth.[13] Two variables which are statistically significant in both models which cause a significant percentage change in the hazard rate for every one-unit increase are Party Competition and full-time legislature. As Party Competition moves from a non-competitive system (1) to a semi-competitive system (2) there is a 70 percent increase in the hazard rate for the Initial Adoption of the UCC, and a 44.8 percent increase in Total Adoption.[14] Similarly, when full-time legislature moves from 0 to 1, there is a 55.6 percent increased hazard rate for Initial adoption and 44.8 percent increase for Total Adoption. This indicates that if all other variables are held at their mean values and full-time legislature was moved from its minimum value, which indicates a part-time legislature, to its maximum value indicating a full-time legislature, we would observe a much quicker adoption of the UCC. These results are encouraging for the hypotheses I have developed. But of course, no definitive results can be drawn after looking at only two models, so I will reserve a comprehensive discussion of the results until all models have been discussed.

Section III B: Common Law Crime

This policy is the only one that requires the state to consciously reject the common law. The other policies are facets of common law, and have implications for common law development, but the policymakers do not have to explicitly state a modification of common law when adopting these other policies even though the policy entrepreneurs recognize the modification that will result. Common law crime requires the state to make the decision on whether they will continue to recognize common law crimes, and for those who do not, require that all crimes be defined by statute or constitutional proclamation. In this model eight covariates are used, five of which reached statistical significance.

As in the UCC models, State GDP and Growth react contrary to expectations. Having addressed this issue in the UCC subsection, little needs to be said here except that the alternative hypotheses suggested may apply here as well, but those hypotheses cannot be adequately tested in the current study. Since these two variables act in the same direction across models, it may be said with some confidence that similar results can be expected for the remaining models. Surprisingly, Full-Time Legislature acts contrary to the findings in tables 3.1 and 3.2. Perhaps this is because abandoning common law crime is done primarily through constitutional revision, and not through statute, which indicates that the role of the legislature may be different and the frequency of sessions may not come into play. But just as there are variables that act contrary to expectations, there are five statistically significant variables that act in the hypothesized direction. ABA, State Population, Particularistic Content, Bills Passed, and Party Competition all exhibit an increasing hazard rate, which means that as the values of these variables increase, the duration before adoption decreases. For example, as the level of Party Competition increases the number of months before policy adoption decreases. The results of the analysis are shown in table 3.3.

Table 3.3. Factors that Influence the Decision to Eliminate Common Law Crime

Variables	*Hazard Ratio (Standard Error)*	*Percentage Change in Hazard Rate*
ABA	1.005* (.0021)	.5
Growth	.962* (.0122)	−3.8
State GDP	.999* (.0000)	−.1
Full-Time Legislature	.772* (.4055)	−22.8
Bills Passed	1.101* (.3090)	10.1
Party Competition	2.059* (.7598)	105.9
State Population	1.002* (.0001)	.2
Particularistic Content	1.002* (.0216)	.2

N = 2150 Log-Likelihood = −46.21 Chi-Square = 296.40
*Significant with One-Tailed T-Test at < .05

Party Competition is the variable which immediately jumps out as being of the most relevance. Since it creates the largest percentage change (105.9) per one-unit change in X, one might be tempted to say that it is the most important, but this is not a conclusion that can be drawn. Since each of the variables is measured on a different scale, their comparability is limited. For instance, if State A has a highly competitive party system it is not necessarily true that it will lead to a shorter duration than State B which is a one-party dominated state since State B may have an ABA score 420 times greater than State A. What should be recognized is that State Population and ABA act in the anticipated direction, and each leads to a modest percentage change, but the potential for increase is much greater with these variables than it is with Growth. The maximum Growth can be is one hundred; this would require a 100 percent increase in government size from one year to the next, but the State Population regularly increases by more than one hundred people and the ABA can on occasion outpace an increase of one hundred. Similarly, Party Competition has a ceiling of 2; its greatest move is from 1 to 3.

Section III C: Sentencing Commission

Table 3.4 gives the complete results of this model, and as discussed in the subsection for common law crime, State GDP has a decreasing hazard rate,

Table 3.4. Factors that Influence the Creation of a State Sentencing Commission

Variables	*Hazard Ratio (Standard Error)*	*Percentage Change in Hazard Rate*
ABA	1.012* (.0028)	1.2
Percent Urban	1.088* (.0218)	8.8
State GDP	.999* (.0006)	−.1
Full-Time Legislature	2.393* (2.0749)	139.3
Number of Judges	1.013* (.0037)	1.3
Judge Selection Method	.811* (.3217)	−18.9

N = 2150 Log-Likelihood = −48.95 Chi-Square = 42.42
*Significant with One-Tailed T-Test at < .05

which means that as the GDP level rises, the more months will pass before policy adoption. As table 3.4 shows, three of the five statistically significant variables act in the anticipated direction. As with the earlier models, the more bar members that reside and practice within a state, the more quickly that state will adopt a policy which works to move the common law system in the direction of a more uniform system, which results in a higher level of certainty. The variable which complements ABA, Number of Judges, goes in the anticipated direction as well, giving more confidence to my interpretation of the ABA variable. Since State GDP and Growth were used to represent similar community features as Percent Urban, there is some hesitation in saying that Percent Urban supports the hypothesis that increased levels of community complexity leads to a more rapid movement away from the common law, even though Percent Urban acts in the hypothesized direction.

We see a similar pattern in these results as we have seen in the others, a modest yet important percentage change in the hazard rate as a result of a unit change in ABA. And while State GDP acts in opposition to original predictions, it acts as expected based on the first three tables, but contrary to original expectations. The new variable, Percent Urban, leads to a nearly 9 percent change in the hazard rate. This means that as the level of urbanization increases by one percentage point, there is a 9 percent decrease in the number of months before a state creates a sentencing commission.

In addition to an EHA, this policy lends itself to a Logit analysis, the results of which complement the findings from the Cox model. Since thirty-one states had not created sentencing commissions by 2002, a dummy variable was created, which is labeled Sentencing Commission. This is a variable in which 1 indicates the state has created a commission, and 0 indicates that no commission has been created. The results of the Logit model are given in table 3.5. As table 3.5 shows, the results of the Logit analysis support the results found in the EHA.

Since the Logit model is not a linear model like OLS, the coefficients are not directly interpretable. The researcher can gain information from the sign which accompanies each variable, but that is about it. In order to provide a meaningful interpretation, the researcher needs to manipulate the values in a way that allows for meaningful interpretation. The last column in table 3.5 gives the probability that a state will adopt a sentencing commission if all values in the model, except for the variable of interest, are held at their mean, and the variable of interest is moved from its minimum to its maximum value. For example, table 3.5 shows that if a state has mean values for all variables except for State GDP, whose value is moved from its minimum to its maximum, the likelihood that state will create a sentencing commission decreases by over 93 percent. Alternatively, if a state with a mean value for all included variables increases its judgeships from the minimum 14 to the maximum 1,479, the likelihood of creating a sentencing commission increases by over 94 percent. This analysis does not lead to any new findings apart from those in table 3.4, but reinforces our understanding of how these variables affect the decision to create a sentencing commission.

Table 3.5. Logit Analysis of State Sentencing Commission

Variables	*Coefficient (Standard Error)*	*Probability*
ABA	.018* (.0076)	.899
Percent Urban	.109* (.0376)	.865
State GDP	−.003* (.0001)	−.935
Full-Time Legislature	1.294 (1.4005)	.135
Number of Judges	.017* (.0071)	.944
Judge Selection Method	−.107 (.7199)	−.018
Constant	−14.397 (5.1715)	

N = 50 Chi-Square = 30.42 Pseudo R^2 = .44
*Significant with One-Tailed T-Test at < .05

Section III D: Civil Procedure Reform

Civil Procedure Reform is a direct adjustment to the common law system of pleading, and the adoption of the Civil Procedure Reform by the states signals the end of common law pleading, as well as the common law distinction between courts of law and equity (Surbin 1987).[15] The results in table 3.6 support the results found in the above subsections. Industrial is the only variable unique to this model and it acts counter to my earlier prediction. Industrial measures the level of industrialization within a state, and is intended to be a complement to the State GDP variable used in the other models. As with State GDP, the hazard rate decreases with increased levels of industrialization. Since there is some similarity between the two variables, perhaps the alternative hypotheses I have offered may apply here as well. Increasing levels of industrialization may signal strength in that state's economy, and a strong economy may be reluctant to change; furthermore, a government which has been successful in promoting a strong economy may be strong enough to resist outside forces that try to bring about change. But since State Population is intended to measure the level of societal complexity, and acts in the anticipated direction, which is opposite of Industrial, it is difficult to be conclusive about the variables which are intended to serve as proxies for societal complexity. While some of the data do not support the original hypotheses, there are certainly alternative explanations for what may cause these effects. Furthermore, little research has been done to create variables which measure the complexity of a society, so it is not surprising that this

Table 3.6. Influence of Selected Variables on the Decision to Adopt Civil Procedure Reform

Variables	*Hazard Ratio (Standard Error)*	*Percentage Change in Hazard Rate*
ABA	1.002* (.0008)	.2
Growth	.982* (.0061)	−1.8
State GDP	.997* (.0009)	−.3
Full-Time Legislature	.848* (.2781)	−15.2
Bills Passed	.961* (.1254)	−3.9
Party Competition	2.256* (.6062)	125.6

N = 2150 Log-Likelihood = −133.652 Chi-Square = 40.65
*Significant with One-Tailed T-Test at < .05

early attempt was somewhat unsuccessful. These results, however, should not completely discount the complexity hypothesis since the descriptive research does support the hypothesis.

A pattern at this point should be clear. For a one-unit increase in X, one observes a greater percentage change in the hazard ratio of Party Competition than for any of the other statistically significant variables. ABA, Growth, and State Population exhibit behavior that has come to be expected. This gives some degree of confidence to the conclusions that are reached in the next section. I would feel a bit uneasy about drawing conclusions if ABA acted in a different direction and at different magnitudes across each of the models, but since there is a high level of consistency for this variable and others, then I may proceed in somewhat safe surroundings, especially when the Number of Judges variable complements these findings. What provides more support to the conclusion drawn from ABA is the descriptive analysis with reference to attorneys that is provided in chapter 2, as well as the historical analysis which follows in chapter 5. Attorneys play a vital role in the adoption of uniform codes. This conclusion is given even more support from the Logit model and the variable Number of Judges. It appears that attorneys are successful policy entrepreneurs. The early organizations that were established to create uniform codes were manned primarily by members of the Bar, and the American Bar Association openly supported the adoption of uniform codes. While I am not willing to call my results on this matter conclusive, I can, with confidence, say that the move toward uniform laws was in large part due to the ABA. Combining the quantitative analysis with the historical analysis, and the fact that the ABA does not hide its position on this matter, we can say that the ABA has been successful in pursuing its agenda with regard to uniform codes.

In addition to being a matter that is heavily influenced by interest groups, political factors are also crucial in understanding when a state acts to adopt a uniform code. Broad policy reforms that do not have an obvious political advantage are generally accomplished when there is a competitive two-party system, as indicated by the Party Competition variable. This hypothesis was put forth in 1960 by E. E. Schattschneider, and finds support in this analysis. The hypothesis offered at the opening of this chapter has found some level of support in that we see that when the political environment is such that interest groups can have a significant influence, the changes made will increase the authority of the government and the influence of the interest group. More support for this conclusion will be given in the next two chapters.

NOTES

1. This is not meant to suggest that there are not important differences among states; if that is what was meant then using the states as a test group would make little sense for this study. What I mean by this statement is that the fifty states share important characteristics that may be difficult, if not impossible, to control the effects of if I were to use a sample of fifty democratic nations. To put it differently, although there are distinct differences between Louisiana and Maine, the gulf is not as wide as if India and Mexico were being compared; therefore fewer statistical controls are required when studying Louisiana and Maine than if one were studying party competition in Mexico and India.

2. Complete support for this hypothesis will not be found until the conclusion of chapter 5. Chapters 3 and 4 will demonstrate what sort of societal and political factors need to be in place to make these changes.

3. These models are also referred to as hazard models, survival models, or duration models.

4. In this study time is measured in months; therefore the duration is the number of months from 1960 to the time of policy adoption. The duration can range from 0–504 months.

5. All states would eventually adopt the entire UCC.

6. A perfectly competitive state receives a score of .500, with a range from .451–.549. A state that leans in one direction will vary between .550–.749 and .450–.251.

7. There has been some controversy over the use of the Ranney Index; I feel that my method addresses many of the concerns.

8. The logic for including these variables is evident if one follows the reasoning for the UCC. A high score for ABA, Growth, State GDP, Party Competition, Full-Time Legislature, and Bills Passed will lead to a higher hazard rate.

9. The scale moves from least influential to most influential: (1) Election (partisan or nonpartisan), (2) Missouri Plan, (3) Appointment (legislature or gubernatorial).

10. This variable was double-checked for accuracy through a data set provided by Laura Langer, accessed through her website http://www.u.arizona.edu/~llanger/NSFSESLANGER.htm.

11. There are four policies but there are five EHA models since the UCC is broken into two categories: Initial UCC and Total UCC. For Sentencing Commissions I will introduce a Logit model since a dummy variable can be created for those states that created a commission and those that have not.

12. "The interpretation of the coefficients with continuous variables is slightly different [from dummy variables]. If one is subtracted from the coefficient and the result is multiplied by 100, then the resulting number gives percentage change in the hazard rate in any given year of rule due to a unit change in the variable" (Bienen and van de Walle 1992, 708).

13. While this small change may seem insignificant, one need only remember that the number of attorneys nearly doubles in every state every ten years. And while the rate has slowed somewhat, it is still a great enough increase to make a significant impact. Furthermore, since this variable is consistent across all models, we can be certain that the number of attorneys in a state has an important impact.

14. This effect is constant, so moving from (2) to a competitive state (3) gives the same effect.

15. A comprehensive history of Federal Civil Procedure Reform is provided in chapter 5 when the Reform is discussed in the context of equity pleading.

4

The Decline in the Use of Juries

Jury trials have been termed the palladium of justice by Leonard Levy, and little dispute is raised over the jury's purpose and its ability to fulfill this function. The criticism of juries is that they are expensive, time consuming, and often unpredictable. Those who want to reform the jury system and restrict the use of the jury system desire a system which is cheaper, more efficient, and more predictable. The empirical research has concerned itself with whether jury reforms have been able to make the court system more efficient and inexpensive with little concern for whether there has been a compromise in the administration of justice. Juries were created as a way for the community to assert its sense of right and wrong and protect against arbitrary decisions by the government. A jury, if properly chosen, is representative of the community, therefore ensuring that the governed have some say in the outcome. As the use of juries declines, so too does the community's involvement in the governing process as it limits the number of avenues available to the general public to participate in government. A decline in juries means that more power is being placed in the hands of judges, court administrators, and lawyers, with less power in the hands of the people. A decline in the use of juries means there are fewer checks on the judicial branch. A decline in the use of juries indicates an abandonment of the common law and the principles it embodies. Scholars interested in issues dealing with the administration of justice, political representation, interest group influence, and the democratic process will find something relevant to their field in this discussion of juries.

Those Englishmen who settled in North America brought with them, among other things, the jury system. The First Charter of Virginia (1606). provided for jury trials, and the colony should

> have and enjoy all Liberties, Franchises, and Immunities within any of our Dominions, to all Intents and Purposes, as if they had been abiding and born, within this our realm of England, or any other of our said Dominions.

In 1641 the Massachusetts Body of Liberties was adopted by the General Court of Massachusetts containing six articles which protect the right to trial by jury. Similar provisions for protecting the jury were codified by the settlers in New Amsterdam, New Jersey, and Connecticut, and the importance of juries was established in Baltimore through common practice. As traditionally conceived, common law served as a consensus building mechanism, a mechanism that also insured that laws would govern and not the capriciousness of those individuals who made up the government. But like much of the common law system, the jury system has undergone some alterations. Even as early as the nineteenth century William Nelson observes that:

> The jury had ceased to be an adjunct of local communities which articulated into positive law the ethical standards of those communities and which in doing so completely dominated the legal system's decision-making processes. (Nelson 1994, 170)

When the American colonies began making a transition toward self-government, they made a concerted effort to protect the jury system. The Declaration of Rights of the First Continental Congress proclaimed:

> The respective colonies are entitled to the common law of England, and more especially to the great and inestimable privilege of being tried by their peers of the vicinage according to the course of law.

These sentiments were echoed by the First Session of the American Stamp Act Congress, and provisions for protecting the jury system had been adopted by nine of the thirteen colonies. The commitment to trial by jury was so strong that it played a role in the decision to take up arms against England. In the list of grievances against King George III, the Declaration of Independence cited, "For Depriving us, in many cases of the benefits of Trial by Jury." When Virginia adopted its state constitution in 1776 there were two sections in its Bill of Rights that protected the jury trial. The desire to establish and protect the jury trial was addressed in the American Declaration of Independence and continued throughout the U.S. Constitution. From the early colonies through the ratification of the Constitution, the commitment to trial by jury was clear, and consistently confirmed.

Perhaps the most recognizable hallmark of the common law system is the jury trial. The jury trial allows the community to sit in judgment on its own, and to make decisions with regard to justice. Elizabeth T. Lear makes the point that the jury system is based on the idea that

> Twelve people, each placing different emphasis on various bits of testimony, remembering statements in different ways, and drawing different conclusions from the demeanor of witnesses, can challenge and refine each other's views. If they are able to arrive at a unanimous decision about "what happened," we feel more confident about their conclusion than we do about the conclusion of one individual who has seen many criminal trials, knows the prosecutor personally, and has the inevitable biases that come with power and experience. (Lear 1993, 1236)

Moreover, the jury was established in Article III, Section 2 of the Constitution to prevent the arbitrary use of government power by allowing ordinary citizens the chance to participate in the process. Alexis de Tocqueville observed that "By obliging men to turn their attention to other affairs than their own, it rubs off that private selfishness which is the rust of society" (Tocqueville 2000, 295). Juries played a central role in the judicial systems and in the writings of the legal scholars that influenced our nation's Founders. Not surprisingly then, the jury system was given a prominent role within our judicial system, through Constitutional Amendments which reinforced its importance. The movement away from jury trials in our federal and state judicial systems which began in the nineteenth century is continuing today. This movement has been given legitimacy by Supreme Court decisions, and the effects of those decisions are seen at the state court level.

This chapter acknowledges that there has been a decreasing use of jury trials at both the federal and state level. The purpose of this chapter is twofold. Section I reviews the cases which authorize courts to limit their use of juries as well as those cases that sanction the limitations placed on the jury's authority. The second section of this chapter offers an empirical investigation into what may contribute to the decreasing use of juries at the state level.

SECTION I: JUDICIAL DECISIONS AFFECTING THE JURY SYSTEM

Clearly the Supreme Court has jurisdiction over matters concerning jury trials, as the issue is a constitutional matter. The question which is raised is, how has the jury trial, and thus the Constitution, been affected by Supreme Court decisions? Has there been a restriction on the use of jury trials? Or, perhaps the decisions have expanded the authority and use of juries. Through an examination of Supreme Court decisions I will show that the Court has restricted the jurisdiction and authority of juries. First I will look at how the Court has created a separate category of crimes known as petty offenses. Petty offenses were in the criminal justice vernacular before the Court used the term, but petty offenses were not used as a filter for deciding which cases had the right to be tried in front of the jury until the Court applied the term. Then I will present an examination of decisions which restrict the authority of juries. This collection of decisions is intended to show how the Court has used its power as Constitution interpreter to decrease the authority of the jury. This section will show that there has been an effort on behalf of the federal judiciary to restrict the role of juries. State judiciaries have taken their cue from the federal level as they recognize that they have the support of the federal judiciary to restrict the use of juries.[1] Section II shows that there has been a downward trend at the state level, and explores the factors that contribute to the trend.

Section I A: Limiting Jury Jurisdiction through Petty Offense Decisions

For the first time, the Supreme Court gave a standard of what constituted a petty offense in *United States v. Baldwin*,[2] and it was decided by the Court that any offense which carried a maximum penalty exceeding six months in prison was considered a serious offense and required the use of a jury to hear the case so long as the defendant did not waive his right to a jury trial. The Court's majority agreed that "In deciding whether an offense is 'petty,' we have sought objective criteria reflecting the seriousness with which society regard the offense, and we have found the most relevant such criteria in the severity of the maximum authorized penalty." The question left open by the *Baldwin* decision was what should become of offenses whose penalty was less than six months in prison. "Subsequent decisions modified this approach to avoid dependence on murky common law precedents" (Butler 1995, 878–79). The modification occurred nearly two decades later in *Blanton v. City of North Las Vegas*.[3] In *Blanton* the Supreme Court handed down a decision which became the standard for differentiating between petty offenses and more serious crimes. The Court said that anything less than six months did not trigger the Sixth Amendment, and therefore a jury trial was not required.

In these cases the Court said that it would rely on community preferences to decide if a case was petty or not, and the gauge for measuring community preferences was the state legislature.[4] Felix Frankfurter and Thomas G. Corcoran give a near complete definition of community preferences that has been used in subsequent Supreme Court decisions:

> In subjecting certain conduct to the summary procedure of magistrates, unguarded by the popular element, there was an exercise of moral judgment dividing behavior into serious affairs and minor deeds. . . . Broadly speaking, acts were dealt with summarily which did not offend too deeply the moral purposes of the community, which were not too close to society's danger, and were stigmatized by punishment relatively light. (Frankfurter and Corcoran 1926, 980–81)

What is established by *Baldwin* and *Blanton* is a system which redefines how community preferences are defined and gauged. Instead of being something which is somewhat obscure, and in fact may change from case to case, the community preference was codified in some sense. Prior to *Baldwin-Blanton*, the Court had set a precedent in *District of Columbia v. Clawans*.[5] The Court decided in *Clawans* that the severity of a statutory penalty could be used to transform an offense from one of petty common law to a more serious offense. In *Clawans* the Court stated that "Doubts must be resolved . . . by objective standards such as may be observed in the laws and practices of the community taken as a gauge of its social and ethical judgments" (301 U.S. 617, 1937). In *Baldwin-Blanton* the Supreme Court decided to abandon the common law tradition even further by using the state legislature as the measure for the preferences of a community. *Baldwin-Blanton* established that if a state legislature required a maximum penalty of six months for a crime, then it would be concluded that the community considered this offense to be serious and a jury trial would be granted.[6]

While 1970 might have been the first time that the Court recognized the state legislature as the measure of the community preferences, and decided that six months was the standard for qualifying an offense as serious, there are decisions which provided precedents for the Court's *Baldwin-Blanton* decisions. One year prior to *Baldwin* the Court said that "In ordinary criminal prosecutions, the severity of the penalty authorized, not the penalty actually imposed, is the relevant criterion" (*Frank v. United States*, 395 U.S. 147, 1969). The decision reached in *Frank* found support in *Duncan v. Louisiana* which said, "The penalty authorized for a particular crime is of major relevance in determining whether it is serious or not and may in itself, if severe enough, subject the trial to the mandates of the Sixth Amendment" (391 U.S. 145, 1968). Also in 1968 the Court decided in *Dyke v. Taylor Implement Manufacturing Co.* that

> Alleged criminal contemnors must be given a jury trial, therefore, unless the legislature has authorized a maximum penalty within the "petty offense" limit or, if the legislature has made no judgment about the maximum penalty that can be

imposed, unless the penalty actually imposed is within that limit (391 U.S. at 291–220, 1968)

In 1974, following *Baldwin* and preceding *Blanton*, the Court decided that "The judgment about the seriousness of the crime is normally heavily influenced by the penalty authorized by the legislature" (*Codispoti v. Pennsylvania*, 418 U.S. 506, 511, 1974). The Court has argued, even before *Baldwin*, that there is a logical connection between the decisions handed down by the state legislature and community preferences. "The relevance of the sentence, as we have seen, is that it shed light on the seriousness with which the community and the legislature regard the offense" (*Cheff v. Schnackenberg*, 384 U.S. 373, 390–91, 1966). While the Court is not far off base in assuming that there is a logical connection between community preferences and action by the state legislature, whether there exists an actual connection is less concrete.

Baldwin-Blanton established a clear line of demarcation between serious offenses and petty offenses. But what happens when there is no statutory mandated penalty? The Supreme Court addressed this problem in 1968 with *Bloom v. Illinois*.[7] *Bloom* says that "When the legislature has not expressed judgment as to the seriousness of an offense by fixing a maximum penalty which may be imposed, we are to look to the penalty actually imposed as the best evidence of the seriousness of the offense" (391 U.S. at 211).[8] The Bloom decision suggests that the state legislature is not always suitable for determining the preference of the community. When this occurs, a judge—independent of the jury—should be placed in charge of determining the community's preference. This is odd given that the original purpose of the jury as to provide the court with some sense of the community because judges were deemed inadequate in this regard. *Bloom* authorizes the judge to decide whether a crime is serious. If the judge decides that the penalty should be less than six months in prison then no jury trial is to be granted, if the penalty imposed is to exceed six months, then the case has to be retried in front of a jury with the defendant already found guilty. This causes obvious complications for due process and double jeopardy, but the Court ignored these complications in 1974 when it reconsidered, and upheld, the *Bloom* decision.[9]

There exist a number of issues with this formulation of petty offenses which potentially violate the authority of the Constitution, how it is enforced and interpreted, and the common law foundations of the Constitution. First, the federal courts are not to be restrained by state laws according to the Constitution and precedent, but the federal courts are subjected to state law under the *Baldwin-Blanton* formulation. Second, relying on state legislatures to decide if there ought to be a jury trial effectively gives the state legislature the power to define the Sixth Amendment. Third, the constitutional grounding of these decisions is unsettled. The decisions made with regard to petty offenses find their justification through precedent, not the Constitution. So instead of relying on a strict interpretation of the Amendments that address jury trials, the Court instead relies on Supreme Court precedent. Last, this allows federal judges to enforce the arbitrary standard of six months on state judges, when in fact that state may or may not consider this standard to be just. This proves a violation of both common law and federalism. Under the common law system the jury was the voice and conscience of the community and it is this understanding which the jury provisions of the Constitution are based upon. This understanding has been altered by the Supreme Court.

Section I B: Further Restrictions on the Authority and Jurisdiction of Juries

The Seventh Amendment states that:

> In suits at common law, where the value in controversy shall exceed twenty dollars, the right of trial by jury shall be preserved, and no fact tried by a jury trial shall be otherwise re-examined in any Court of the United States, than according to the rules of the common law.

However clearly stated the Amendment may appear, the reach of the Seventh Amendment has been severely limited through judicial decisions in at least two ways.[10] First, Congress may assign administrative agencies the task of adjudicating violations of federal statutes. Second, the Seventh Amendment does not extend to cases brought against the federal government. This section will discuss in detail the court decisions that established the precedents for these two restrictions on Seventh Amendment rights. In addition to Seventh Amendment restrictions, the use of acquittal enhancements by the judiciary has limited the jury's ability to decide either fact or law. While acquittal enhancements have Seventh Amendment implications, the issue casts a broader net which is not limited to a single Amendment. An analysis of *United States v. Vernon Watts*[11] will address this issue. By limiting the application of the Seventh Amendment and the use of acquittal enhancements, the courts have limited the jurisdiction and authority of juries.

Section I B.1: Administrative Agencies

The first time the Court faced a Seventh Amendment objection to adjudication by administrative agencies was in *National Labor Relations Board v. Jones and Laughlin Steel Corporation*.[12] Jones and Laughlin Steel Corporation argued that an NLRB order to provide back pay as a remedy was equivalent to damages, thus creating a right to a jury trial under the Seventh Amendment. But without citing a single authority, the Court held that

> The instant case is not a suit at common law or in the nature of such a suit. The proceeding is one unknown to the common law. . . . The contention under the Seventh Amendment is without merit. (301 U.S. 1, 1937)

Not until 1974 was the *Jones and Laughlin* decision tested. In *Curtis v. Loether*[13] the Court said:

> *Jones and Laughlin* merely stands for the proposition that the Seventh Amendment is generally inapplicable in administrative proceedings, where jury trials would be incompatible with the whole concept of administrative adjudication. (415 U.S. 194, 1974)

One must at least question the reasoning of how a constitutionally established right can be limited by an agency with only statutory authority. In *Atlas Roofing Co. v. Occupational Safety Commission*[14] the Supreme Court upheld the precedent established in *Jones and Laughlin* and *Curtis*. In *Atlas Roofing Company* the Court rejected the Seventh Amendment challenge to a statutory scheme that allowed an administrative agency to impose civil penalties on violators. A unanimous Court held:

> at least in cases in which "public rights" are being litigated . . . the Seventh Amendment does not prohibit Congress from assigning the fact finding function and initial adjudication to an administrative forum with which the jury would be incompatible. (430 U.S. 442, 1977)

More than one hundred federal statutes allow civil penalties to be imposed in excess of twenty dollars without a jury trial,[15] statutes clearly in violation of the Seventh Amendment, yet still upheld by the Supreme Court as constitutional statutes.

In *Commodity Futures Trading Commission v. Schor*[16] the Court held that the Seventh Amendment would not apply to an administrative adjudication even if a jury trial would be required on the same issue in federal court. The Court had established the precedent that the Seventh Amendment must not only consider the nature of the issue to be resolved, but the forum in which it is to be resolved. However, it is unclear what other forum the Founders would have had in mind. These cases add up to an alarming conclusion, which is, no Seventh Amendment check on Congressional authority to assign agency adjudicating functions exists.

Section I B.2: Federal Immunity

One of the most well established and least challenged areas of Seventh Amendment restriction occurred in *Galloway v. United States*,[17] in which the Supreme Court decided that the right to a jury trial does not extend to suits against the federal government. In *Galloway* the Court said:

> The suit is one to enforce monetary claim against the United States. It hardly can be maintained that under the common law in 1791 jury trial was a matter of right for persons asserting claims against the sovereign. Whatever force the Amendment has therefore is derived because Congress, in the legislation cited, has made it applicable. (319 U.S. 388)

This essentially means that the actions of the federal government are not reviewable by a jury, unless the federal government gives its consent. This interpretation of the Seventh Amendment finds support in *Gliddon Company v. Zdanok*[18] and *McElrath v. United States*.[19] In *United States v. Testan*[20] the Court's majority said, "the United States, as sovereign, is immune from suit save as it consents to be sued . . . and the terms of its consent to be sued in any court define that court's jurisdiction to entertain the suit" (424 U.S. 399). Even in cases where Congress has waived the federal government's immunity from a civil or criminal suit, it does not necessarily waive its right to avoid a jury trial. In *Lehman v. Nakshian*[21] the Court wrote:

> When Congress has waived the sovereign immunity of the United States, it has almost always conditioned that waiver upon the plaintiff's relinquishing any claim to a jury trial. . . . But even if the legislative history were ambiguous, that would not affect the proper resolution of this case, because the plaintiff in an action against the United States has a right to a trial by jury only where Congress has affirmatively and unambiguously granted that right by statute. (453 U.S. 156, 1981)

Section I B.3: Acquittal Enhancements

In *Vernon Watts* the Court upheld the judiciary's long-held practice of revising jury decisions with regard to penalties assessed in both criminal and civil cases. The *Vernon Watts* decision authorizes judges to increase the sentence originally handed down by a jury. This decision was made pursuant of the United States Sentencing Guidelines.[22] The decision to enhance a sentence, or punishment of any kind, rests on the judge's discretion. If the judge finds that the defendant's relevant conduct demands an increased sentence then he may enhance the sentence handed down by the jury. The defendant's relevant conduct extends beyond the crime which he was convicted of, and includes offenses which the defendant was acquitted of.[23] The precedent for this decision goes back to 1935 when the Court decided in *Dimick v. Schiedt*[24] that judges are authorized to decrease damages without the use of a jury. In *Dimick* the Court said:

> A careful examination of the English reports prior to that time fails to disclose any authoritative decision sustaining the power of an English court to increase, either absolutely or conditionally, the amount fixed by the verdict of a jury in an action at law, with certain exceptions. (293 U.S. 474, 1935)

It was these "certain exceptions" that subsequent Court decisions keyed in on. The exceptions granted were not specifically enumerated by the Court in *Dimick*, though examples were provided. Once authorization has been granted to decrease the damages, it was only a short step to concluding that judges have the authority to increase damages as well. In *Dimick* the Court denies that the natural corollary to decreasing a fine is increasing it. But *Dimick* laid the groundwork for enhancements by allowing for exceptions to its decision by providing the justification for a judge's ability to alter a jury's punishment. It was not until *Vernon Watts* that we see the Court uphold a judge's ability to increase a jury's punishment. The Court rested its opinion on statute law, which it says "codifies the longstanding principle that sentencing courts have broad discretion to consider various kinds of information" (117 U.S. 633, 1997). The Court goes on to cite the relevant statute:

> No limitation shall be placed on the information concerning the background, character, and conduct of a person convicted of an offense which a court of the United States may receive and consider for the purpose of imposing an appropriate sentence. (The *Vernon Watts* Court citing 18 U.S.C. Section 3661)

The *Vernon Watts* decision is somewhat unique in that it does not rely on precedent for its reasoning; in fact, it seemingly violates the controlling precedents. *Vernon Watts* may be a punctuated equilibrium in the evolutionary history of Supreme Court precedent. We have seen this before—the Supreme Court handing down a decision without consulting any earlier case even where applicable precedents exist.[25]

The cases I have reviewed in Sections I A and I B show that the Court has taken an active role in limiting the role and jurisdiction of juries. By providing this review, the stage has been set for the empirical analysis in Section II. Without reviewing the relevant case law justification for the decreasing use of juries, one may be left to wonder why the Court has not taken action to rectify state violations of constitutional guarantees. But a review of Supreme Court cases allows one to see that the Court has taken an active role in limiting juries as well as setting precedents for other courts who wish to legitimize their decisions to decrease the use of jury trials. That is to say, if a strict construction of the Constitution were granted with regard to the sections that deal with juries, one would anticipate an increase in the use of juries as there are more trials year after year. But we have witnessed a decrease at both the federal and state level. In order for this to occur, there must first be authorization from the Supreme Court that limiting the use of juries is constitutional. What follows in Section II is a time-series analysis of which institutional and environmental factors contribute to the varying use of jury trials at the state court level.

SECTION II: TIME-SERIES ANALYSIS

Section I provided evidence to support the claim that action has been taken that allows the jurisdiction and the authority of the jury to be restricted, but the analysis cannot end there. Section II provides a state-level time-series analysis to bring about an understanding of what factors contribute to the decline in the use of civil and criminal juries. Section II A will provide an explanation for the chosen model specifications. Section II B will give the results of the time-series analysis along with a description of the dependent variables.

Section II A: Reasoning behind the Chosen Model Specification

Except for Crime Rate, all of the explanatory variables used in this chapter were used in at least one model in chapter 3. Crime Rate is a measure compiled by the Federal Bureau of Investigation made available through their website which gives the number of violent and nonviolent crimes committed in a state per one hundred thousand people. The explanatory variables used in this chapter will range from 1976–2002, whereas those used in chapter 3 ranged from 1960–2002. The inclusion of Crime Rate makes sense, as an increasing crime rate is often cited as the culprit for an increasing caseload, which means that plea bargaining is often used instead of trials (Alschuler 1979; Langbein 1992 and 1979; Smith 1986; Fisher 2000). "In most criminal cases, plea bargaining is necessary and inevitable—at any rate, that is the view of nearly all knowledgeable scholars and practitioners and much of the public at large" (Schulhofer 1984, 1037). Based on these past studies that have used single county samples to conduct their research, it is expected that there is a negative relationship between jury trials and crime rate. As the crime rate increases, the percentage of jury trials will decrease.

The literature that deals with jury trials tends to agree that the more judges there are the more often jury trials will occur in relation to bench trials (Schulhofer 1984; Fisher 2000). Schulhofer and Fisher offer complementary findings though their articles are released sixteen years apart, giving support that their claims stand the test of time. Also the literature predicts that the size, and growth, of government should be positively correlated to the percentage of jury trials (Fisher 2000).[26] These predictions make sense intuitively. First, if there are more judges, then the caseload per judge will not be as heavy. Second, if a state government is big, or rapidly growing, then it can be reasoned that the state is willing to expend its resources on staff, and the lack of government resources and staff are the most commonly cited reasons why juries are not used more often.

Of course the common law literature draws different conclusions regarding these two factors (Nelson 1994; Surbin 1987; Manning 2001). The more judges the stronger the influence within the government, from that state's bar. As was argued in chapter 3, increased levels of bar involvement will lead to a decrease in the strength of the common law system, in this case, jury trials. Second, the more government growth the more weakened the common law system (Manning 2001; Rosen 1994; Nelson 1994). As has been argued at some length, the common law system acts as a sort of brake on government encroachment; thus, government growth and common law are almost opposing forces. Formal government structures require codified rules and rigid procedures; these characteristics are contrary to common law. Therefore, the common law literature would predict that the greater the size of government, the less jury trials will be utilized. I will use the Number of Judges to measure the number of judges within a state, and Growth to measure the growth of a state's government.

State GDP is a variable that was used in most of the models in chapter 3, so the reasoning behind it here should already be clear. State GDP represents a measure for the growing complexity within a state. Combined with Percent Urban and Growth, the actual effect of the growing complexity of a society can be accurately triangulated. William Nelson makes the point that economics is a leading cause in the changes felt by the increasing complexity of society. A shift occurs in society when it grows larger and more complex socially and economically.[27] In reference to the growing government and increasingly complex and economically centered society in nineteenth-century Massachusetts Nelson writes:

> government was becoming increasingly able to compel recalcitrant minorities to obey rules of law they found objectionable. . . . America had ceased to be a mechanism for the preservation of local power and the building of local consensus or to be a mirror of stable and widely shared ethical values. . . . More often, however, the function of the law was to resolve disputes among individuals seeking control over a particular economic resource. (Nelson 1994, 163–64)

The point Nelson makes, and the hypothesis tested by using Growth, State GDP, and Percent Urban, is that as society and government grow, the consensus-making mechanisms of the common law system are abandoned.

The remaining two variables are ABA and Judge Selection Method. ABA is used and measured in the same way here as it was in chapter 3. The role of the ABA in the movement away from the common law system is undeniable when its history is traced in a descriptive fashion (Surbin 1987). I will add to what is known about the role of the ABA and its involvement with the transformation of the common law system by empirically testing the effects of its involvement in this chapter as well as chapter 3. ABA measures the level of involvement of the bar within a state, and Judge Selection Method measures the amount of involvement from the bar in selecting its judges. These two variables are expected to have a negative impact on the percentage of jury trials.

Having established the reasoning behind the explanatory variables used, the new dependent variables also require some attention. The new dependent variables are Criminal Jury and Civil Jury.

Criminal Jury: These data were provided by the National Center for State Courts (NCSC). The data are the total number of bench trials for each of the twenty-one states represented in the sample, as well as the total number of jury trials per state. The states were solicited by the NCSC to report their data, and it was up to the states to report. This means that the sample is not random. To arrive at the percentage of jury trials per state, bench trials and jury trials were added together and the sum was divided by the number of jury trials. Since this is a cross-sectional time-series data set, each state has a value for each year.

Civil Jury: These data are derived from the same source and in the same manner as Criminal Jury. The only difference between the two variables is that civil jury provides the percentage of jury trials for civil trials, whereas Criminal Jury is concerned with criminal trials. Also, the states which are in each data set are different. Since the NCSC relies on the states to report the data, not all states track and report this sort of data. Therefore, the states which compose Criminal Jury do not necessarily populate the Civil Jury data set.

Section II B: The Empirical Results

From 1976 to 2002 the average rate of decline, across the twenty-one states in the sample, for the use of juries in civil cases was nearly 5 percent and 7 percent for criminal cases, while the number of bench trials remained relatively stable, showing only a slight downward trend in some instances. This is consistent with the academic literature which has been tracking the decline of juries, and trials in general. Most of the studies which deal with the decreasing rate of jury trials have focused on the role played by plea bargaining (Holmes, Daudistel, and Taggart 1992). In fact, the results from these studies have so consistently confirmed the effects of plea bargaining on jury trials that some states have been moved to ban the use of plea bargaining despite its constitutional validity (Rubinstein and White 1979). Unfortunately this chapter does not integrate plea bargaining into the model as the data are simply not available. Not only are there no state-level data available that span the years in this study, the states that do make these data available offer the data for only a single year, and those data are admittedly incomplete. This being said, however, plea bargaining is not the only factor which has affected the downward trend in jury trials (Elder 1989). But outside of recognizing that factors other than plea bargaining exist, the literature does not have a study which has taken a rigorous quantitative approach at the state level. Any state-level study deals with only a single state. This study uses twenty-one states, focusing on factors other than plea bargaining.

Section II B.1: Results

Initially, the most striking feature of the findings in tables 4.1 and 4.2 is the modest impact of the variables in explaining the percentage of jury trials. While these results are not the basis for paradigm shifting research, we may take comfort in knowing that the findings have strong theoretical grounding as they relate to common law, and they are supported by the findings in chapter 3.

The first variable that should be considered is Crime Rate. Nearly all of the literature that studies the decreased use of juries cites the increase in crime rate as being the prime culprit. These findings suggest that Crime Rate has no statistical bearing on the percentage of criminal jury trials in the twenty-one states of this sample. Next, attention should be drawn to Percent Urban, as the literature cited would suggest that urbanization and jury trials would be negatively related. Table 4.1 suggests otherwise, and the variable in table 4.2 does not reach statistical significance, so can neither be used to support nor discount the current literature. Another variable that does not reach statistical

Table 4.1. Criminal Jury

Variables	*Coefficient (Standard Error)*	*Z-Statistic*
ABA	−.00024 (.000059)	−4.03
Growth	.0000347 (.00017)	.2
State GDP	−.00133 (.00066)	−2.04
Crime Rate	−.0062 (.0065)	−1.06
Number of Judges	−.0000196 (.0000874)	−.22
Judge Selection Method	.007 (.017)	.41
Percent Urban	.0040 (.0012)	3.34
Constant	.458 (.116)	

N = 567 Overall Adjusted R^2 = .01

significance is Number of Judges. The standard literature has suggested that the more judges there are, the more manageable the caseload, and the more likely the jury system will be maintained. My hypothesis suggests that the more judges there are the stronger the influence of the legal profession and hence fewer jury trials are expected. Neither hypothesis finds support through these data.

The variable which drew the most interest in the last chapter draws attention here as well. ABA is negatively correlated with both criminal and civil jury trials. The more practicing members of the state bar there are in a state, the less frequently jury trials will be used. This is consistent both with the literature cited and with the findings in chapter 3. As the hallmark of the common law system, juries should react in the same way as the other measures of common law. Furthermore, the ABA has released statements and studies arguing for restrictions on jury trials, indicating that they support the decline in the use of jury trials (1983, 1984, and 1992). Once one spends a little bit of time thinking about how the system is arranged this makes sense. If plea bargaining is the substitute for jury trials then the power shifts from juries and judges into the hands of lawyers. During a plea bargain, the attorneys are the ones who make the decision on what justice is by deciding what charges a defendant is guilty of, and what sentence should be served or what damages paid in the case of a civil dispute. Judges must approve the decision, but this is generally a formality with a judge giving the rubber stamp. Second, if a bench trial is the alternative then it makes sense for lawyers to want a judge to make the decisions so they can avoid the capricious nature of a jury. Judges have track records which make them somewhat predictable; juries have no track record and are often unwieldy, making an attorney's job difficult. But what makes these findings so surprising is that juries are so institutionalized through tradition and the U.S. Constitution that it would seem they would be the one feature of the common law system to be steadfast in the face of adversity. What is observed is the influence of legal profession on the structure and practice of the legal system, so much so that across all the models, the ABA measure is the only one to reach statistical significance and act in the same direction.[28]

A critic of these findings may look at table 4.2 and take notice of the unanticipated direction of Judge Selection Method and refute this claim. Critics should remember that judges have only limited discretion in deciding when to grant a jury trial. The theory suggests that the stronger the influence of the ABA, the more likely that state is to have practices which violate traditional common law procedures. That influence can manifest itself in a number of ways, not just in the trial setting. Second, all judges are drawn from the state bar, even those judges who are elected; therefore, one would expect almost no difference between states with different selection methods. We would expect judges to manifest different types of behavior based on selection methods, but perhaps not in this case. Finally, this is the only model which gives this result for Judge Selection Method. In the other models that use Judge Selection Method, the variable fails tests of statistical significance.[29]

The Growth variable reaches statistical significance for Civil Juries only and State GDP for Criminal Juries only. Since these two variables are intended to measure the same phenomena from different angles, these results generate a mixed reaction. In the first place, one may say that we cannot rely on the results of these two variables to draw any conclusions since they are different measures of the same thing and act in different ways by not reaching statistical significance in the same model. I suggest that what is more important is that both variables have a negative relationship to the percentage of jury trials. The more complex society gets, the less frequently jury trials are used. It only makes sense that if juries are used to gauge the sentiment of the community then we would want them to be used even more frequently since gauging the sentiment of the community would presumably become more difficult as the complexity of the community grows. But, as juries are a component of the common law system, and that system tends to deteriorate with growing societal complexity, these results act exactly as anticipated. A word of caution, however: the Growth variable acted contrary to common law

Table 4.2. Civil Jury

Variables	*Coefficient (Standard Error)*	*Z-Statistic*
ABA	−.000031 (.000007)	−4.15
Growth	−.0008 (.0002)	−4.44
State GDP	−.000017 (.000015)	−1.17
Crime Rate	−.000012 (.0065)	−1.60
Number of Judges	−.00018 (.00015)	−1.17
Judge Selection Method	.0034 (.020)	1.71
Percent Urban	−.0003 (.0011)	−.28
Constant	.59 (.110)	

N = 567 Overall Adjusted R^2 = .006

scholars' predictions in chapter 3, so conclusions regarding the variable should be slightly guarded.

CONCLUSION

Combined with chapter 3, this chapter sheds more light on the dismantling of the American common law tradition and the factors that have facilitated its dismantling. It should not be startling to any thoughtful person that the legal community would have the greatest impact on the development of the legal system, since they are the group who is the most involved with that system. What should be startling is that they have been so successful. As a government institution, the court system was designed to be isolated from the influences of a single interest group. Furthermore, the balance of the government system rests on the ability of the courts to remain unbiased so that they may check the actions of the executive and legislative branches. The common law system is the foundation for how the court system was originally conceived. The common law system represents the rule of law, and a check on government infringement. Common law is a consensus building mechanism in the community so that the decisions made will have the force of the people. Thus, the common law system has been compromised by the influence of a select minority, and this violates the principles of both common law and our constitutional framework.

NOTES

1. I make the argument that the Supreme Court has set up a supportive environment for courts to limit the use of juries, which is not the same thing as saying that the Supreme Court has led the movement decreasing the role of juries and because of their actions, other courts have relied less on juries.

2. 399 U.S. 66 (1970).

3. 489 U.S. 538 (1989).

4. The Supreme Court had relied on the term community preference as early as 1969 in *Frank v. United States* 395 U.S. 147 (1969).

5. 300 U.S. 617 (1937).

6. In some sense this is upside down. Under a common law system the jury was the measure of the community's preferences. So without examining any further, it can be tentatively concluded that the traditional role of the jury in the common law system was completely disregarded by 1970. Furthermore, *Baldwin-Blanton* allows the legislature to have control of the jury jurisdiction by lowering the maximum penalty for crimes that it thinks should not be heard in front of a jury.

7. 391 U.S. 194 (1968).

8. Refer also to the discussion on *Dyke*.

9. *Taylor v. Hayes*, 418 U.S. 488 (1974).

10. I had considered a third category which deals with the Court's failure to extend the Seventh Amendment to the states. Since the Court has extended the Bill of Rights to the states through its interpretation of the Fourteenth Amendment, it is peculiar that it holds the Seventh Amendment uniquely from the other nine Amendments in the Bill of Rights. But since the Seventh Amendment did not ever apply to the states according to the Court, then the Court has not restricted the jurisdiction in this case, it has simply failed to apply it to the states; see *Walker v. Sauvinet* 92 U.S. (12 Otto.). 90 (1876). This is a distinct but relevant distinction.

11. 117 U.S. 633 (1997).

12. 301 U.S. 1 (1937).

13. 415 U.S. 189, 194 (1974).

14. 430 U.S. 442 (1977).

15. 132 Congressional Record 24867-69 (1986).

16. 478 U.S. 833 (1986).

17. 319 U.S. 372 (1943).

18. 370 U.S. 530.

19. 102 U.S. 426.

20. 424 U.S. 392. The Court found support for its reasoning in *Testan* in *United States v. Sherwood*, 312 U.S. 584.

21. 453 U.S. 156 (1981).

22. *Federal Sentencing Guidelines Manual* (1997).

23. This does not authorize the judge to look at new facts which were withheld from the jury.

24. 293 U.S. 474 (1935).

25. Refer back to *Jones and Laughlin* and *Brown v. Board of Education*, (349 U.S. 294, 1955).

26. Fisher (2000) offers a nearly comprehensive review of the literature surrounding jury trials. The conclusions he reaches complements what is considered now to be common knowledge. Thus, citation to Fisher (2000) is sufficient as it encapsulates most of the important studies that preceded his.

27. The justification for these measures is provided in chapter 3, as well as the justification for all of the other variables used in this chapter except for Crime Rate and the Dependent Variables.

28. An alternate explanation might be to suggest that as the number of attorneys increases so too does docket size, making the need to abandon jury trials necessary since jury trials take up so much time, thus making the conclusion that the ABA has less political weight than I suggest. But, since I can draw on findings in chapter 3 and ABA reports that suggest the ABA is in favor of restricting juries, I feel confident in my explanation.

29. I would like to make a definitive statement about power shifting into the hands of judges when juries are not used, but unfortunately I cannot. While judges do benefit from receiving more trials than juries, which gives them more opportunity to exert power, without the inclusion of plea bargaining this is only a tentative conclusion since in plea bargaining the power shifts to attorneys and limits the power of judges.

5

Equity, Sovereign Immunity, and Consequences

A brief history of equity was given in chapter 1, as well as a review of the most influential studies to date on the topic. This chapter will use court decisions made in equity to test the projections made by the Anti-Federalists and the Federalists during the ratification debates. The primary concern of the Anti-Federalists was that the federal courts would be able to usurp the law by using its power in equity, and the Federalists rebutted by saying the power in equity was necessary to make sure that justice was served in a case where a literal application of the law would be too stringent. Section I of this chapter will begin with a history of equity in the United States which will show how the legal profession has been out in front leading the change. Section I will also provide a more expansive definition of equity that builds on what has already been discussed in chapter 2. Section I concludes with an analysis of the portions of the ratification debate that focus on the power of equity, linking the debate to relevant contemporary concerns. The central theme of the ratification debates as they concern equity is that resting the power of equity and law in the same court will allow judges a more expansive power than they ought to have, which will result in their infringement on the rights of the states and the other branches. In addition to the problem posed to federalism and separation of powers, mixing equity with law will lead to the rule of judges and not the rule of law. Sections II, III, and IV will set forth testing the claims made by each side during the ratification debates. Section II will discuss what rules courts apply in distinguishing between suits of law and equity. Section III will discuss federalism and separation of powers with respect to the Court's use of equity jurisdiction. Section IV discusses the how the law and equity distinction has been confused by, and led to confusion in, the debate over the distinction between courts and administrative agencies.

SECTION I: THE DEFINITION OF EQUITY, THE RATIFICATION DEBATES, AND THE LEGAL PROFESSION

Section I A: Definition

If one were looking for origin, one would settle on Aristotle's discussion of equity in the *Nicomachean Ethics*. He notes:

> All law is universal but about some things it is not possible to make a universal statement which shall be correct. In those cases, then, in which it is necessary to speak universally, but not possible to do so correctly, the law takes the usual case, though it is not ignorant of the possibility of error. And it is none the less correct; for the error is not in the law nor in the legislator but in the nature of the thing, since the matter of practical affairs is of this kind from the start. . . . And this is the nature of the equitable, a correction of law where it is defection owing to its universality. (Aristotle 1934, 1137 b)

In a separate text Aristotle revisits the issue of equity in the *Rhetoric* when he tries to clarify the principle of equity by saying:

> For that which is equitable seems to be just, and equity is justice that goes beyond the written law. These omissions are sometimes involuntary, sometimes voluntary, on the part of the legislature . . . for life would not be long enough to reckon all the possibilities. If then no exact definition is possible, but legislation is necessary, one must have recourse to general terms. (Aristotle 1926, 1374a)

The debt owed to Aristotle is clearly seen when one examines the writings of thinkers who are considered to be influential men in the progression of the strain of Western legal thought that influence the Americans. Take, for instance, the writing of Cicero, who said of equity:

> A perversion of justice, some extremely clever but harmful interpretation of a statute, also is a frequent cause of wrongdoing. Hence we have the saying *Summum Ius Summa Iniuria*, "Extreme legality is the worst law," a proverb become a cliché in daily use. (Cicero 1952, 1.6.19)

Aristotle's influence is not lost on St. Germain:

> It is not possible to make any general rule of the law but that it shall fail in some case. And therefore makers of law take heed to such things as may often come

> and not to every particular case for they could not though they would and therefore to follow the words of the law were in some case both against justice and the commonwealth: wherefore in some cases it is good and even necessary to leave the words of the law, and to follow that [which] reason and justice requires and to that intent equity is ordained (St. Germain 1974, 97)

This line of thinking is repeated by English jurists such as Coke, Bracton, and Kames. The reasoning behind equity is quite clear, and was made, at least in part, by Publius during the ratification debate. It must be recognized by any reasonable person that legislatures cannot make laws that will be universally just and applicable, making some other mechanism necessary to protect against injustice while not entirely repealing statutes as statutes are not entirely invalidated by encountering a single instance of inapplicability.

According to John F. Manning, the purpose of equity is best seen when examining its application by English judges, whom he credits for serving as the baseline for the American understanding of judicial power.

> Under the authority of that doctrine [equity], English judges had often extended statutes beyond their plain terms in order to make them more coherent expressions of purpose, and cut back others to avoid inequitable results that did not serve the statutory purpose. (Manning 2001, 8)

This point is made salient when one refers back to Plowden's note in *Eyston v. Studd*:

> So that a man ought not to rest upon the letter only . . . but he ought to rely upon the sense, which is temperated and guided by equity, and therein he reaps the fruit of the law. . . . And in order to form a right judgment when the letter of a statute is restrained, and when enlarged, by equity, it is a good way, when you peruse a statute, to suppose that the law-maker is present, and that you have asked him the question you want to know touching the equity, then you must give yourself such an answer as you imagine he would have done, if he had been present. (75 Eng. Rep. 695, 699, 1574)

When applied, equity allows the courts to extend a statute to reach omitted cases, an extended group, or to allow exceptions to a statute when it would inflict a punishment which would be counter to the intent of the legislature that passed the law. At the heart of equity is the idea that statutory law can be too rigid. In some instances it may be too strict; in others it may be too lenient. When applying the equity principle judges try to gain some sense of what the legislature's intention was, to determine what an appropriate application of the law would be. Equity is in place because judges understood that certain laws, when applied, would not bring about the results that the statute had intended. Furthermore, there are some cases that escape the scope of a statute, but that statute may be applied through equity jurisdiction. Just as legislatures cannot be expected to anticipate every scenario in which a statute will apply, they cannot determine how it should be applied in every situation. Michael C. Dorf concludes that through equity jurisdiction courts become partners with the legislature.

> Students of constitutional law are familiar with an alternative conception of democracy in which courts play a vital role as partners with, rather than mere servants of, the legislature. (Dorf 1998, 19)

While the acceptance of Dorf's thesis is less than universal, it makes some sense in the way equity was intended to work in the American system, and not just equity, but the common law in general. Dorf's thesis may lead to a violation of the separation of powers principle which lies at the heart of the Constitution, and it may be overly optimistic in thinking that the judiciary and the legislature do not have to be at odds in order to protect liberty. The point that should be taken from Dorf's thesis is that equity, as it was originally understood, was to be complementary of the legislature, and in no way authorized the making of positive law to be put into the hands of judges.

Section I B: The Ratification Debate and Contemporary Concerns

There seems to be little disagreement over the principle of equity. The problem lies in its application and the potential it has to be a destructive force. Of the opponents of the powers of equity granted to the federal judiciary Brutus was the most vocal during the ratification debates. Brutus, probably Robert Yates, also provides the most cogent argument, outlining the potential threats of the judiciary as designed by the Constitution. When referring to Article III, Section 2 of the Constitution Brutus says:

> This article, therefore, vests the judicial with a power to resolve all questions that may arise on any case on the construction of the constitution, either in law or in equity. . . . This article vests the courts with authority to give the constitution a legal construction, or to explain it according to the rules laid down for construing a law. . . . By this they are empowered, to explain the constitution according to the reasoning spirit of it, without being confined to the words or letter. (*Brutus XI*, January 31, 1788 in Ketcham 1986, 294)

Brutus was concerned with the authority granted to the courts, not because of the powers enumerated, but because the powers enumerated were vague. He saw the danger lying in the court's ability to make decisions in both law and equity with no clear split between the two. It was through the power of deciding cases in equity that Brutus was so concerned, since equity jurisdiction would allow the court to interpret in such a manner that the intent may be violated, and there was no power which could check the court's interpretation of the Constitution. Brutus's understanding of equity allows the court authority to reach beyond the letter of the law, and this, in part, is what breeds his pessimism regarding the judiciary as designed by the Constitution.

> "From this method of interpreting laws," says Blackstone, "by the reason of them, arises what we call equity"; which is thus defined by Grotius, "the correction of that, wherein the law, by reason of its universality, is deficient;" for since in laws all cases cannot be foreseen, or expressed, it is necessary, that when the decrees of the laws cannot be applied to particular cases, there should somewhere be a power vested of defining those circumstances, which had they been foreseen the legislator would have expressed; and these are the cases, which according to Grotius, "*lex non exacte definit, sed arbitrio boni viri permitted.*" (*Brutus XI*, January 31, 1788 in Ketcham 1986, 295)

Brutus's definition of equity differs little from the definition given earlier in this chapter, but he contends that the authority granted through equity, and specifically the way it is granted in the Constitution, can lead to negative consequences for federalism.

Let it be understood that Brutus did not oppose equity, but he opposed it when unchecked and when the potential existed for it to be applied to legal and constitutional matters. Furthermore, he saw the Constitution as establishing an energetic national system that would eventually swallow the states. He envisioned a Court manifesting this vision through its use of equity discretion.

> The judicial power will operate to effect, in the most certain, but yet silent and imperceptible manner, what is evidently the tendency of the constitution—I mean, an entire subversion of the legislative, executive and judicial powers of the individual states. Every adjudication of the Supreme Court, on any question that may arise upon the nature and extent of the general government, will affect the limits of the state jurisdiction. In proportion as the former enlarge the exercise of their powers, will that of the latter be restricted. (*Brutus XI*, January 31, 1788 in Ketcham 1986, 296)

His vision of a national government seeking to centralize power was based on his idea that men who held government office were power mongers who sought office in order to exert control over the system. Thus, it is only natural that institutions, when populated by these men, would act to centralize power as the men in those offices would seek to consolidate power into their own offices, and it was within the power of the federal government to successfully fulfill this vision. He interpreted the Constitution in such a way that the men in government would be able to undermine the state governments through constitutional interpretation; thus the Court had the greatest ability to threaten the states.

This prediction of how the judicial system would work is quite different from the overt argument made against Brutus by Alexander Hamilton, specifically in *Federalist Papers* 78–83). Alexander Hamilton as Publius wrote:

> In the first place there is not a syllable in the plan . . . which directly empowers the national courts to construe the laws according to the spirit of the Constitution, or which gives them any greater latitude in this respect that may be claimed by the courts of every state. (*Federalist* 81, 419)[1]

Hamilton reminded the people of New York that the "particular powers are marked out in the Constitution" (*Federalist* 80, 413). Hamilton argued that the Constitution was "one which contains certain specified exceptions to the legislative authority," and that the role of the courts was such that they provided "an intermediate body between the people and the legislature in order, among other things, to keep the latter within the limits assigned to it" (*Federalist* 78, 404). It is to be understood, as Hamilton argued, that the Court would not exceed its enumerated powers, and would serve as a check on the legislature to protect the interests of the people.

The primary role of the judiciary was to provide a check on the other branches, according to Hamilton. In fact, the argument made throughout by Publius is that the strength of the government is in its structure, and its success as an instrument of liberty and security rests on its system of checks and balances.

> Until the people have by some solemn and authoritative act annulled or changed the established form, it is binding upon themselves collectively, as well as individually; and no presumption, or even knowledge of their sentiments, can warrant their representatives in a departure from it, prior to such an act. (*Federalist* 78, 403)

The proper role of the judiciary, therefore, is to help preserve that structure. In order to ensure that the judiciary would "avoid an arbitrary discretion" it was created as "the least dangerous branch . . . beyond comparison the weakest of the three departments of power" (*Federalist* 78, 402). However, these assurances did little to assuage the concerns of Brutus and the other Anti-Federalists.

The concerns expressed by the Anti-Federalists did not come out of thin air. John Dickinson reflected on the courts in Pennsylvania and concluded, "every court there is a court of equity . . . every verdict is a confused mixture of private passions and popular error, and every court assumes the power of legislation" (Colburn 1962, 450–51). Nor was Brutus the only Anti-Federalist to see the potential problems associated with allotting powers of law and equity to the same court. Samuel Bryan, writing as Centinel, addressed the citizens of Pennsylvania in an attempt to warn them about the potential dangers hidden within the Constitution. With reference to Article III, Section 1, where the powers of the judiciary are initially defined, Centinel writes:

> The objects of jurisdiction recited above, are so numerous, and the shades of distinction between civil causes are oftentimes so slight, that it is more than probable that the state judicatories would be wholly superceded; for in contests about jurisdiction the federal court, as the most powerful, would ever prevail. Every person acquainted with the history of the courts of England, knows by what ingenious sophisms they have, at different periods, extended the sphere of their jurisdiction over objects out of the line of their institution, and contrary to their very nature; courts of a criminal jurisdiction obtaining cognizance in civil causes. (*Centinel* 1, October 5, 1787 in Ketcham 1986, 233)

Clearly the concern over the jurisdiction between criminal and civil cases is motivated by the law and equity jurisdiction which resides in the same courts at the federal level. The concerns expressed by Centinel are those that are expressed by all who are concerned with the construction of the federal judiciary, which are, the federal courts will assume the authority of the state courts and centralize power in the national government. Through their power to interpret the intent of the Constitution and their jurisdiction over law and equity cases which gives them the power to make such interpretations, the power of the state governments can be substantially compromised if not altogether destroyed. The Anti-Federalists seem to follow the logic of Lord Kames, who wrote:

> To determine every particular case, according to what is just, equal, and salutary, taking in all circumstances, is undoubtedly the idea of a court of equity in its perfection, and had we angels for judges, such would be their method of proceeding, without regarding any rules—but men are liable to prejudice and error, and for that reason cannot safely be trusted with unlimited powers. Hence the necessity of establishing rules to preserve uniformity of judgment in matters of equity as well as common law. (Kames 1972, 112)

Alexander Hamilton rebuffed the projections made by the Anti-Federalists by reciting the checks placed on the judiciary. His most relied-on defense of the judiciary was that their income was controlled by the legislature, they could be impeached, they were required to rest their decisions on standing precedent, and they were without the power of purse and sword. They relied on the legislature for funding and the executive for enforcement. Equally important, courts must wait for cases to come to them; if an issue was not raised before the courts, then they could not address the issue. But in direct response to those who cite the court's jurisdiction as being potentially problematic, Hamilton responded as Publius saying that the jurisdiction

> is declared by the constitution to comprehend certain cases specifically specified. The expression of those cases marks the precise limits beyond which the federal courts cannot extend their jurisdiction; because the objects of their cognizance being enumerated the specification would be nugatory if it did not exclude all ideas of extensive authority. (*Federalist* 83, 435)

The Anti-Federalists were unconvinced even by this line of reasoning. Brutus reasoned that the judicial power would use its equity jurisdiction to "explain the constitution according to the reasoning spirit of it, without being confined to the words or letter" (*Brutus XI*, January 31, 1788 in Ketcham 1986, 296). In his most direct refutation of the claims made by Hamilton in *Federalist* 83, Brutus says that the powers of the judiciary "are conceived in general and indefinite terms, which are either equivocal, ambiguous, or which require long definitions to unfold their meaning" (*Brutus XI*, January 31, 1788 in Ketcham 1986, 296). But the Federal Farmer provides the most cited rebuttal against Publius with regard to the judiciary and equity jurisdiction.

> It is a very dangerous thing to vest in the same judge power to decide on law, and also general powers in equity; for if the law restrain him, he is only to step into his shoes of equity, and give what judgment his reason or opinion may dictate . . . we have no precedents in this country, as yet, to regulate the divisions in equity . . . therefore, in the supreme court for many years equity will be mere discretion. (*Federal Farmer Letter III*, October 10, 1787 in Storing 1981a, 2.8.185)

The ratification debate obviously ended with the ratification of a new U.S. Constitution. In this respect the Anti-Federalists lost since they were fighting against ratification. But the question which has never been resolved is who won the argument? That is, whose assessment about the potential development of the Constitution was more accurate? This is the question which motivates the remainder of this paper. A review of how the Supreme Court has exercised its equity jurisdiction will provide insight into resolving the dispute between the Federalists and Anti-Federalists. There have been relatively few studies which have tackled this issue. Most of the relevant studies have already been cited with respect to the codification debate. What these scholars have noticed is that there is a direct link between codification and the blurred line between law and equity (Manning 2001; Laycock 1990, 1991, 1993, and 2002; McDowell 1982 and 1993; Rosen 1994; Surbin 1987). These studies show that there has been a significant shift in the legal profession as a result of the changing distinction between law and equity that resulted from the adoption of the Federal Rules of Civil Procedure in 1938. Mark D. Rosen writes:

> Among other things, codification has bureaucratized the law, thereby inhibiting critical examination of the adversary system and the role of the jury, and has advanced an ethic of atomism at the expense of community solidarity in legal fields as diverse as contracts, evidence, and criminal law. (Rosen 1994, 1119)

While the literature has provided extensive documentation on how the legal system has evolved, the literature has failed to include a detailed discussion of Supreme Court decisions. What is lacking is a review of decisions which document how the Supreme Court has used its equity discretion before and after 1938. Furthermore, the current studies are more concerned with what these developments mean for the legal profession and the operation of the judiciary than what the implications are for other parts of society. The review I provide adequately fills the first of these holes, while drawing inferences into the second hole without providing a definitive answer to what impact these decisions have had on society and government at large.

Section I C: History of the Federal Rules of Civil Procedure

Article III of the Constitution authorizes the federal courts to exercise powers of both law and equity. With the passage of the Judiciary Act of 1789, these powers were given a statutory foundation to complement their constitutional origin. Until the mid-nineteenth century, beginning with the Field Code, federal district courts had a law side and an equity side, helping to keep the two areas of law separate as they had been separate in the common law system. The Field Code dealt specifically with the states and by 1911 only seven states had separate courts of law and equity, and today only four states have separate courts of law and equity. At the federal level, the merger of law and equity was not completed until 1938 with the passage of the Federal Rules of Civil Procedure. As chapters 3 and 4 demonstrated, the legal profession is a conductor of change within the specified areas of common law, and the unification of law and equity is no different.

In 1906 Roscoe Pound addressed the annual ABA convention in support of procedural reform which would give more authority to equity. Pound supported a breakdown in common law procedure with the substitution of equity-based rules. Pound thought that common law focused too extensively on the individual and not enough on the community.[2] Pound thought that it was the technicalities in the current procedural norms of 1906 that stood in the way of justice, and substituting those procedures with uniform ones based in equity would lead to a higher level of justice. As a result of Pound's speech to the ABA, they established a Committee to Suggest Remedies and Formulate Proposed Laws to Prevent Delay and Unnecessary Cost in Litigation. The ABA movement that followed Pound's path accepted his equity based methods. In 1912, the ABA Committee of Fifteen, which Pound was a part of, successfully lobbied the Supreme Court to adopt the Federal Equity Rules of 1912, which replaced the Equity Rules of 1842. Under the new rules, technical pleadings and demurrers were eliminated and the right to amend was liberalized.

Five years after Pound's famous address, Thomas Shelton picked up the torch and began pushing Congress to pass the Enabling Act authorizing the Supreme Court to promulgate uniform federal rules. Shelton is an interesting figure in the story since he reversed his position on uniform procedural rules between 1910 and when he was appointed the first chairman of the ABA Committee on Uniform Judicial Procedure in 1912. Under his direction, states began adopting their own simplified rules based on the recommendations of the ABA and Shelton's Committee on Uniform Procedure. The Enabling Act Movement and the Equity Rules of 1912 were strikingly similar in content in that they both sought to simplify procedure and increase the role granted to equity. The ABA's Enabling Act garnered a groundswell of support among the legal community, including Chief Justice Taft, who encouraged the federal adoption of procedural rules that merged law and equity in order to create a more simplified system.

In 1922 Shelton testified in front of the House Judiciary committee on behalf of the Enabling Act, saying that the procedural rules in place were too technical.

> This is one of the things that is making Bolshevists in this country; that frequently, a sensible man, a business man, a practical business man, sits in the courtroom and sees his case thrown out on a technicality that he can not understand, and does not know why it is necessary.

This part of the ABA's argument on behalf of the Enabling Act is what generated the highest levels of support. Everyone seemed to be in favor of simplifying the system. The Conformity Act, which the Enabling Act was to replace, made it difficult to practice in federal court as one did not know what procedural law would apply, and thus the risk of having a case thrown out on procedural grounds was high.

After the groundwork had been laid by Pound and Shelton, Charles E. Clark finished the job that was begun by Pound and Shelton. In 1935 Clark made a move from the Dean of Yale Law School to Reporter of the Supreme Court Advisory Committee and drafted the new Federal Rules of Civil Procedure that would go into effect in 1938. Clark made no excuses for being in favor of a more simplified system of pleading that would end many of the arbitrary procedural lines and categories. And while Clark may not have had the charisma of Shelton or Pound, he had the fortitude to see the job through. It was through his efforts in lobbying Congress and rallying the legal profession that would bring the Enabling Act to fruition. Clark commissioned reports, and wrote his own, that showed the injustice bred by the current system of procedure. Finally, in 1938 with the passage of the Federal Rules of Civil Procedure, the legal profession got what it had been fighting for, for over thirty years—a new procedural system that merged law and equity. While this story is certainly not complete, a brief examination of the roles played by Pound, Shelton, and Clark shows that it was the efforts of the legal profession that brought about the Federal Rules of Civil Procedure which further blurred the line between law and equity, a line that the federal courts had been obscuring for some time.

After surveying the definition, debates, and history surrounding equity in the United States, it is time to move on and discuss how equity jurisdiction has developed through Supreme Court decisions in which it has applied its equity jurisdiction. The following sections show how the Court has used its equity jurisdiction to increase the jurisdiction of the federal courts and the scope of the federal government relative to the states.

SECTION II: HOW THE FEDERAL COURTS HAVE EXPANDED THE SCOPE OF THEIR INFLUENCE THROUGH THE USE OF EQUITY JURISDICTION

This section has a direct bearing on the concerns of the Anti-Federalists. This section will explain how the court has used its equity jurisdiction to expand its authority by reviewing cases in which the courts made decisions in equity and not law. The bulk of the analysis will focus on how the irreparable injury rule has developed and been applied. The irreparable injury rule suggests that when a remedy provided by the law is insufficient in remedying the injury of the plaintiff, the Court has the authority to look outside the legally prescribed remedy, thus using its equity jurisdiction.

> It is hornbook law that equity will not act if there is an adequate remedy at law. This rule is rooted in the beginnings of equity as a royal dispensation from the failings of the common law. Inadequate remedy at law began as a rationale for the equity court's separate existence and consequently became the rationale for defining and limiting the court's jurisdiction. For if the equity court sat to correct the common law's inadequacies, it followed that there was no need for equity in cases in which common law was satisfactory. (Laycock 2002, 370)

The irreparable injury simply states that when the law is unable to repair the injury or when an injunction is necessary to prevent an action which would be irreparable by law, equity jurisdiction may be enforced. In addition to the irreparable injury rule there is the practice of determining the "adequacy of the law" when deciding if a case falls under the control of legal or equitable jurisdiction. The "adequacy of law" rule is quite similar. It states that if there is no adequate remedy at law then equity jurisdiction may be used to provide an adequate relief. The adequacy of law is a less stringent test and is more often used where the law is clearly defined, whereas the irreparable injury rule is used when law in an area is vague or when an injunction is requested. While the irreparable injury rule is the most tractable forum for seeing the development of equity jurisdiction, other cases will be used to give more breadth to the types of cases used which show the development of the Court's current application of equity. This section will set the stage for the two that follow by showing that in general, the federal court's power has been expanded through its use of equity jurisdiction, and Sections III and IV will give evidence of this in specific arenas.

Section II A: Irreparable Injury and Adequacy Rules

Douglas Laycock has provided the legal field with extensive research on how the irreparable injury rule has been applied in various settings, and how equity jurisdiction has developed as a result of how the irreparable injury rule has been utilized. Laycock makes the observation that

> It should not be surprising that equity interpreted the irreparable injury rule in ways that expanded its jurisdiction. Once equity established a substantive equitable right, it enforced that right without any inquiry into whether some legal right might be just as good in a particular case. Similarly, once equity began to enforce a right or grant a remedy, it continued to do so even if the same right or remedy later became available at law. (Laycock 2002, 381)

This is a powerful statement in the sense that it suggests the ability of the court to ignore statute law if precedent and common usage are in place. That is, even if Congress conforms to the practices of the court, the court still retains its prerogative.[3] What's more, this statement suggests that equity jurisdiction allows the court to act in the very way Brutus said it could and Publius said it would not.[4]

The Court teetered on the brink of radically increasing its equity jurisdiction in 1946. In *Porter v. Warner*[5] the Court argued that when the "public interest is involved in a proceeding" the equitable powers of the federal judiciary "assume an even broader and more flexible character than when only a private controversy is at stake" (328 U.S. 395). This reasoning was used in the subsequent desegregation cases. In *Brown v. Board of Education* (1954 and 1955)[6] the Court handed down an opinion that expanded the definition of what cases fell under the Court's equitable jurisdiction. The Court concluded that segregation imposed an injury that was irreparable by law, and required an equitable remedy in order to provide a just remedy. It included not just the individuals who filed suit in its case, but an entire aggrieved social class who suffered sociological and psychological damage. This Court used both prongs of equity jurisdiction: (1) to provide remedy which is not provided by the law, (2) to expand the sphere of the remedy to include more than just the litigants of the case. This expanded equity jurisdiction became solidified in subsequent decisions, including *Swann v. Charlotte-Mechlenburg County Board of Education*.

In 1971 the Supreme Court handed down a decision which further expanded its power to grant equitable relief; the case was *Bivens v. Six Unknown Named Agents*.[7] Justice Brennan, writing for the majority, concluded that "federal courts may use any available remedy to make good the wrong done." In *Bivens* the Court decided that it had the authority to grant remedies that were not explicitly granted by congressional statute; this decision was made in an effort to "effectuate the congressional policy underpinning the substantive provisions of the statute" (*Bivens*, Justice Harland concurring). The Court's interpretation of its own powers to grant certain remedies is the most intriguing part of this decision. Justice Brennan makes the point of saying that "For we have here no explicit congressional declaration that persons injured by a federal officer's violation of the Fourth Amendment may not recover money damages from the agents." The interesting phrase is "may not." This seems to say that the Court has authority to do anything which is not explicitly denied to them by Congress. It seems that the Court could have easily denied a monetary reward since they were not given the explicit power to do so in this case. One of the points that I will make throughout this chapter is that the Court has been inconsistent on this matter. In some instances it says that it cannot do something which Congress has not directly granted it the authority to do as in *Alexander v. Sandoval*, and in other instances it makes a determination that is consistent with *Bivens*. What results from this inconsistency is a Court who makes its own decisions on what it can and cannot do, and it is its use of equity that makes it possible.

Alexander v. Sandoval[8] provides an important example of how the Court has recently applied its equity jurisdiction to expand the authority of the federal government. *Alexander* is commonly discussed alongside *Bivens*, as the two address similar matters and arrive at varying conclusions. Whereas *Bivens* grants relief because Congress does not explicitly restrict such relief, *Alexander* refuses relief because Congress does not explicitly grant the Court power to do so. Justice Scalia writes for the majority in *Alexander* that:

> Neither as originally enacted nor as later amended does Title VI display an intent to create a freestanding private right of action to enforce regulations promulgated under Section 602. We therefore hold that no such right of action exists.

If one recalls Justice Brennan's position, one will notice a striking inconsistency between the two positions. The one consistency between the two opinions that fits with a more general trend is that the court has taken it upon itself to determine when and how it is to interpret Congress's meaning in statutes.[9] Not that this is surprising; the tradition of judicial review has become quite an accepted practice. But since neither of these cases deals explicitly with the constitutionality of a law, it is curious as to why the Court would try to interpret the intention of Congress and not simply apply the statute. There is no strict formula for deciding when equitable relief is acceptable. The irreparable injury rule and the determination of adequacy of legal remedies are obviously no serious restraint in the decision-making process since both seem relatively malleable. Furthermore, the *Alexander* decision represents a blow to common law tradition. The traditional view held that the statute created the right to sue for damages, and the common law created the remedy unless a remedy had been negated through statute. *Alexander* overrides this practice.

In *Carlson v. Green*[10] the Court handed down a decision consistent with *Bivens* in stating that "victims of a constitutional violation by a federal agent have a right to recover damages." The Court has made the *Bivens* precedent narrowly applicable. At least six other cases have sought relief under the provisions established by *Bivens* and have been denied monetary relief.[11] In these six cases the defendant was not an agent, but an agency, therefore stating that an individual within the government could be held liable, but the government itself could not. This is somewhat disconcerting for those worried about increasing nationalism, especially when the Court has decided that entities at the state level can be held liable. The precedent was established in 1824 by

Osborn v. President of the Bank of the United States,[12] which was followed by Congressional action with the passage of the Civil Rights Act of 1871.[13] Furthermore, the willingness of the Court to hold state agencies accountable and make them suffer the burden of providing relief is most cogently seen in the desegregation cases of *Bolling v. Sharpe* and *Brown v Board of Education, Topeka*. Had these schools been an extension of the national government, there is little evidence to conclude that the same decisions would have been made, especially when we see in *Chappell v. Wallace* that the Court is unwilling to end discriminatory practices by the national government against black sailors as late as 1983.[14]

The Court has successfully established its ability to decide cases in equity when legal remedies are available, even if the decisions are somewhat inconsistent in their application. Additionally, the indictment by Laycock that the Court does not look for legal remedies once it has established equitable remedies for a particular set of cases finds support in *Estate of Cantonia v. Sindel*.[15] In *Estate of Cantonia* the Court confirms the ability of courts with both equity and law jurisdiction to invoke equitable principles despite the existence of an adequate remedy at law. Furthermore, once a court establishes its jurisdiction it will retain jurisdiction until it decides all of the issues adequately and fairly between the parties. Moreover, courts with both jurisdictions may adjust equities without rigid adherence to any form and may shape the remedy to meet the demands of justice. As we have seen, however, the common law principle of stare decisis demands that rigid principles be followed in that like cases get treated in a like manner in order to protect justice. The Court seems to be saying in *Estate of Cantonia* and through its use of equity powers that this sort of restriction is unnecessary.

One factor that has allowed for the expansive use of equity jurisdiction is the established meaning of the term adequacy. A legal remedy is defined as adequate if it is as comprehensive and just as the equity remedy, and it is the court who decides if the legal remedy is adequate. There have been nearly thirty decisions at the federal level that support this definition of adequate.[16] This definition has been used in the Supreme Court and supported at the trial and appellate levels. There are several powerful features of this definition and its application. First, it allows courts to define their own jurisdiction. This is both powerful and surprising considering that it is Congress who is given the power to make decisions concerning the jurisdiction of the judiciary by the Constitution. Second, it has facilitated the merger of law and equity. The common law divide between courts of law and equity has been so blurred that it barely exists, and this has been the case for some time. In fact, there is evidence to support the claim that there is little understanding by lawmakers what the two jurisdictions actually are. In *Mertens v. Hewitt Associates*[17] Justice

Scalia openly asserted this position. He said that the line between law and equity as understood in 1791 is no longer clear to lawyers and members of Congress, and therefore any definition of equitable relief established by Congress through statute could not be relied upon for guidance. Instead, statutes that mention equitable relief should be interpreted as meaning "those categories of relief that were typically available in equity." These categories of course have been established by the courts. Justice Douglas makes an equally compelling argument for the fusion of law and equity when he asserts in *Edelman v. Jordan*[18] that "There is nothing in the Eleventh Amendment to suggest a difference between suits in law and suits in equity, for it treats the two without distinction." Last, there has been little observable backlash over the application of the court's equity jurisdiction. Congress has made no significant effort to rein in the power of the court's equity discretion; more likely is the case that Congress has left certain acts open to the Court's discretion.

SECTION III: FEDERALISM, EQUITY, AND THE IMPACT OF IMMUNITY

The Constitution leaves open to interpretation the issue of federalism and where the lines ought to be drawn between state powers and national powers. Section III A will discuss an area of law which has not been traditionally treated in relation with the federalism issue: immunity. I will show how the Court slips seamlessly between law and equity to give itself, the executive branch, and the federal government immunity which is not based on the Constitution or statutory law. Only the legislature is said to derive its immunity directly from the Constitution, whereas judicial and executive immunity have become law through precedent which was established by the Court using its equity jurisdiction. The Eleventh Amendment provides immunity for the states. Yet the review of cases that I provide will show that the level of immunity the states are granted has been limited through the Court's application of the Civil War Amendments, specifically the Fourteenth Amendment. While the states have lost a substantial part of their immunity, the protection granted to the federal government, and especially the courts, has seen a marked increase.

Section III A: The Issue of Immunity

The Court has no constitutional grounding for granting itself, its officers, or the executive branch immunity.[19] More importantly, it does not pretend to. Only legislative immunity is backed by the Constitution, found in Article I,

Section 6. What is found in the case of judicial immunity is that judges decide that if a judge commits an error it must either apply the irreparable injury rule, or find that the law provides an inadequate remedy. Thus, the question is thrown into equity jurisdiction. When the question is considered in equity, the judiciary is not restricted by law, and is free to grant itself immunity from cases decided in equity, on the basis that immunity allows them to perform their job properly. Eventually the immunity becomes law, as precedent has to some degree become considered law. Judges are able to then derive immunity from precedent and apply it to both law and equity cases. So even when statutory law, if applied, would find a judge guilty of a crime, judges may call on precedent to free them of this restraint, thus leaving the possibility for negative ramifications on separation of powers, federalism, and the rule of law. This also allows the federal government to increase its own sphere of power relative to that of the states since no state has successfully recovered damages from the national government when immunity can be granted to the national government. Second, immunity has been given to state officials, but not as extensively as it has been given to national officials, therefore setting the precedent that members of the national government are in some ways superior to state officials. Evidence for these claims will be borne out in the following analysis.

Section III A.1: Judicial Immunity

Alexander is certainly consistent with the tradition of immunity found in other Supreme Court cases. Immunity in this sense means that the sovereign, when serving in its official capacity, cannot be sued without its consent. In *Stump v. Sparkman*[20] a long-standing precedent was supported which stated that

> a general principle of the highest importance to the proper administration of justice that a judicial officer, in exercising the authority vested in him, [should] be free to act upon his own convictions, without apprehension of personal consequences of himself. (*Bradley v Fisher*, 80 U.S. (13 Wall) 335, 347 (1872) as quoted in *Stump*)

The Court found more support for judicial immunity from Congress, who did not explicitly eliminate such immunity (or confirm it) in 42 U.S.C. Section 1983. Strikingly enough, the Court decided in *Stump* that in cases of judicial immunity, as Justice White writes:

> the scope of the judge's jurisdiction must be construed broadly where the issue is the immunity of the judge. . . . A judge is absolutely immune from liability for

> his judicial acts even if his exercise of authority is flawed by the commission of grave procedural error. . . . Despite the unfairness to litigants that sometimes results, the doctrine of judicial immunity is thought to be in the best interests. (*Stump* 435 U.S. 349)

Should we conclude then, that when a judge acting in his official capacity faces a penalty, the Court has full discretion on the matter of immunity in order to ensure that the judge does not suffer any damages? Even when justice is compromised at the expense of the litigants, should judges be immune in a nation that prides itself on being governed by laws and not by men? As has been seen elsewhere, the Court has decided that it should restrict its jurisdiction when a private citizen is at risk, but in the case of a judge, the Court ought to broaden its jurisdiction. What is true in this case and will be true in the following cases that deal with the issue of immunity is that through the equity jurisdiction that immunity comes about. In *Stump*, the litigant had originally filed seeking a legal remedy against the judge. The Court decided that a citizen could not receive adequate relief from the law when it was a judge who was at fault for the crime inflicted on the citizen. Thus the decision was decided in equity, and immunity was granted to the judge, as if somehow this was a more adequate remedy for the plaintiff. Even when the rule of law is applicable, immunity is granted to a government official acting in his official capacity through the Court's equity jurisdiction.

Bivens, and the cases which hold it as the controlling precedent, recognize that most government employees receive only qualified immunity, but decisions which support the principles of *Stump* place judges, legislators, and presidents in a different category by giving them what often amounts to absolute immunity. However, of the four types of immunity, judicial, executive, congressional, and state, judicial immunity is the most extensive. A mother of three criminal defendants wrote objectionable letters to the judge hearing the case and the judge found her in contempt and sentenced the mother to thirty days in jail. She sued on the basis that state law prohibited the judge from punishing out of court contempt. In *Adams v. McIhany*[21] the Fifth Circuit decided against the mother despite the fact that the judge acted contrary to state statute law; the court understood that it could broadly construe its jurisdiction to protect the immunity of a judge. Even when a judge, in the midst of a trial, plots strategy with a prosecutor in the prosecutor's hotel room, the 10th Circuit found that the judge was immune to the charges brought against him.[22] The verdict in *Malina v. Gonzales*[23] protected a judge who illegally used a flashing red light to pull a car over in a fit of road rage, but did not protect the act of road rage. Malina, not knowing it was a judge in the car with a flashing red light, did not pull over. Three hours later the judge sent a police officer to his house to bring Malina in to the judge's chambers. The judge charged him with six criminal acts. It was decided by the Fifth Circuit that the judge's actions on the freeway were not immune, but sending Malina to jail was an immune act. Each of these cases was initially filed seeking a legal remedy. Legal jurisdiction was denied by the court, and the decision was made in equity. This is an important point to recognize. The common practice before 1938, and before the Field Codes for that matter, was that litigants would choose which forum to file in, and only equity jurisdiction could be denied in favor of a legal remedy. If a case was filed seeking a legal remedy it was to be decided in law; it was only a claim made in equity which could be denied on the basis that there was a legal remedy.

Judicial immunity extends to the actions of officers who act directly under the direction of a judge. In *Mireles v. Waco*[24] a judge ordered two police officers to use excessive force to bring a lawyer into his courtroom; when Waco brought a suit against Judge Mireles, the Court found him immune. *Briscoe v. LaHue*,[25] *Wagshal v. Foster*,[26] and *Roland v. Phillips*[27] each establishes the immunity of an officer acting under the direction of a judge. Unfortunately for court reporters, they are not immune.[28] Certainly some will recognize the danger in protecting an officer who acts in a violent manner under the direction of a judge, but alarmist reactions are not necessary. What is more important is that it is recognized that the common thread that ties all these cases together is the Court's equity jurisdiction. In each of the cases I have cited that deal with judicial and officer immunity, there was violation of a statute law. Thus, to establish immunity in each of these cases, equity jurisdiction was chosen over the legal remedy. Furthermore, the only recent cases that deny immunity are cases that deal with state-level judges.[29] I have come across no case that allows for a federal judge to be prosecuted when that judge is acting in a judicial capacity, or does not consent to being prosecuted.

Section III A.2: Legislative and Presidential Immunity

The Supreme Court has read into Article I, Section 6 of the U.S. Constitution, which states "for any Speech or Debate in either House, they shall not be questioned in any other place," that federal legislators are to be immune from lawsuits. Legislative immunity has not faced many challenges, but those challenges are usually brought by the United States. There are more instances of legislative immunity being refused than there are judicial immunities, and this may be due in part to having the United States as the plaintiff. *Eastland v. United States Serviceman's Fund*[30] generally serves as the controlling precedent for legislative immunity. The Court decided in *Gravel v. United States*[31] that a Senator and his staff were protected from prosecution if they were caught going through, and making public, confidential Pentagon Papers, but they were not immune from being prosecuted for publishing those same papers. Also, the Court decided in *United States v. Brewster*[32] that legislators who received bribes were not immune from prosecution. There is no reason why legislative immunity appears to be less extensive than judicial immunity; nor does the Court address the topic. In fact, the Court states that legislators enjoy more immunity than judges. But there are more instances of immunity being limited in the case of legislators than there are of it being limited for judges. Furthermore, immunity for legislators is derived from the United States Constitution, not equity jurisdiction, which means it has a legal grounding, and not on the Court's ability to maneuver successfully between law and equity. This is an important point to recognize since the Supreme Court has taken it upon itself to invoke equity jurisdiction in deciding a number of these cases. It is equally important to recognize that the constitutionally derived immunity for legislators has more restrictions than the judicial immunity derived from precedent.

The Court has held that no other official is as indispensable as the president, and has distinguished the president from governors, cabinet officers, and presidential aides. In *Nixon v. Fitzgerald*,[33] the Court held that the president is absolutely immune from suits for damages for any action taken in his official capacity. But, the president is not wholly immune from the judicial process. In *United States v. Nixon*[34] the Court unanimously enforced a subpoena against the president. The *United States v. Nixon* case dealt with no trivial matter. The subpoena was issued in a criminal prosecution of some of the president's aides, to obtain tapes of the president's conversations. Congressional reaction to the evidence disclosed pursuant to the subpoena forced the president to resign.[35]

The president is not immune from suit for acts not in his official capacity. In *Clinton v. Jones*[36] the Court said that the principal rationale for official immunity is inapplicable to unofficial conduct.[37] In this case the Court decided that such a suit would not interfere to any substantial degree with the president's duties, even though just fifteen years earlier in the *Nixon* case they based their decision on the idea that lawsuits against the president should not be allowed because they would be too great of a distraction. What's more, had the Court followed the precedents outlined for judicial immunity, it could have decided these suits in equity had it so chosen. By putting the case into equity jurisdiction, immunity could have been more easily granted. But the Court chose no such action.

Section II A.3: State Immunity

Before the passage of the Eleventh Amendment, the delegates at the Constitutional Convention in Philadelphia recognized that the states needed some sort of protection against lawsuits. Even Alexander Hamilton said that "It is inherent in the nature of sovereignty not to be amenable to the suit of an individual without its consent" (*Federalist* 81: p. 418). But, fears materialized early on in the absence of a formal restraint on the ability of private citizens to sue state governments. In *Chisholm v. Georgia*[38] two citizens from South Carolina, acting as executors of a British creditor, filed suit against Georgia. In 1793 the Court decided that the suit was consistent with Article III, Section 2, which gave the federal courts jurisdiction over controversies "between a State and Citizens of another State." To protect state sovereignty against the centralizing tendency of the federal courts, and to protect the states against an onslaught of citizen suits, Congress and the states ratified the Eleventh Amendment, which overturned *Chisholm*. Despite the clear wording of the Eleventh Amendment, "The Judicial power of the United States shall not be construed to extend to any suit in law or equity, commenced or prosecuted against one of the United States by Citizens of another State, or by Citizens or Subjects of any foreign state," the Court has interpreted the Amendment in such a way that has limited state immunity.

While the state may not be sued in its own courts, suits may be brought in another state. A suit against Texas may be brought in Louisiana, and the Supreme Court has held that this is not a violation of the Eleventh Amendment. This sort of suit has been raised, and the Supreme Court has upheld the right to sue one state in another state's court. In *Nevada v. Hall*[39] the Court ruled that, in a tort action against Nevada arising out of a traffic accident occurring in California, California need not give full faith and credit to Nevada's statutory limitation on liability for injuries caused by Nevada state employees. Moreover, the Court has decided that the Fourteenth Amendment supersedes the Eleventh Amendment in certain cases, thus narrowing the scope of state immunity. Suits are allowed against state officers who are charged with violations of due process under the Fourteenth Amendment. In *Ex Parte Young*[40] and *Traux v. Raich*[41] the Court decided that an officer acting illegally is functioning as an individual rather than a state official. What is unique about this sort of legal reasoning is that it does not transfer to the decisions I reviewed above, the decisions which provide immunity to federal officers who violate due process and judges who enjoy absolute immunity.[42] What's more, the Supreme Court has taken the authority away from the state to define its own agencies in an effort to limit the amount of immunity states are granted. In *Pennhurst State School and Hospital v. Halderman* the Court said that even though state law enjoined two institutions which made them state agencies, the federal court must treat them as two separate entities of one which was not a state agency and therefore was not under the protection of state immunity as outlined in the Eleventh Amendment.[43]

The problems that have been presented have not been lost on the Court either. While the Court has not dealt extensively with the role immunity plays in federalism, it has recognized the role the federal government has played in limiting state immunity through the Fourteenth Amendment. Justice Rehnquist, in his dissent in *Rome v. United States*, says that principles of federalism

> that might otherwise be an obstacle to congressional authority are necessarily overridden by the power to enforce the Civil War Amendments "by appropriate legislation." Those amendments were specifically designed as an expansion of federal power and an intrusion on state sovereignty. (446 U.S. 156, 179 1980)

The Court has hinted in *orbiter dicta* and in a number of other decisions, that Congress has the power to abrogate the Eleventh Amendment and allow for states to be sued in federal court without the state's consent.[44] This point is made more salient by Justice Stevens's dissent in *Pennhurst State School and Hospital*:

> The rule the majority creates today serves none of the interests of the State. The majority prevents federal courts from implementing State policies through equitable enforcement of State law. Instead, federal courts are required to resolve cases on federal grounds that no State authority can undo. Leaving violations of state law unredressed and ensuring that the decisions of federal courts may never be reexamined by the States hardly comports with the respect for States as sovereign entities commanded by the Eleventh Amendment.

Immunity seems little more than an artifact of the confusion and manipulability of the equity-law distinction. While immunity has been codified in several places, it is capable of being overridden by judicial interpretation. The level of immunity rests on the interpretation of the Court, even in cases where the guidelines for immunity are clearly stated. Where immunity is not specifically granted it can generate the principle by shifting from law to equity, then relying on precedent in subsequent cases as has been the case for the judiciary and the president. In those instances where immunity is constitutionally derived, the Supreme Court has been able to circumvent the power of the Constitution by choosing to give one part more authority than another as has been the trend with the Eleventh and Fourteenth Amendments. With respect to the legislature, the Court has often granted immunity, but in matters of civil disputes, legislative immunity has been chipped away. In *Gravel* and *Brewster* the Court was able to simultaneously treat civil and criminal concerns, a practice restricted by common law tradition, but allowed when the line between law and equity is blurred. Except for the judiciary, in each case where equity jurisdiction is exercised in decisions of immunity, the Court has limited immunity which has resulted in an increase of its own authority relative to the other branches and the authority of the national government relative to the states.

SECTION IV: THE COURTS, ADMINISTRATIVE AGENCIES, AND EQUITY

Some litigants file suits to bypass administrative agencies, seeking to enjoin proceedings before the agency or to present their case to a court instead of an agency. In order for a litigant to successfully complete this maneuver, they must show that they have exhausted all administrative remedies, or they must invoke the primary jurisdiction of the agency. That is, when a claim is pending that an administrative agency has jurisdiction over, administrative remedies must be exhausted, but when no claim is pending, primary jurisdiction must be invoked. So in either case, administrative remedies must be exhausted before a court can handle the case, under the exhaustion rule. The exhaustion rule began as an application of the irreparable injury rule, stating that courts would issue an injunction only if the administrative remedy would be inadequate. However, there are several exceptions to the exhaustion rule under which the courts invoke their authority to hear a case. Section IV A will give a survey of the cases that have established the exhaustion rule and how the rule of exhaustion conflicted with standing precedent that governed the division of law and equity. I will show how the matter of dividing law and equity became even more confused when courts and agencies clashed over jurisdiction. Section IV B will discuss the exceptions to the exhaustion rule. This section will show that courts have used these exceptions to increase their own authority over an area of cases that had originally been under the jurisdiction of administrative agencies. While common law sympathizers may think this a proper role for the courts, I make the point that it is not the intention of the courts to prop up an ailing common law system, but instead it is a turf war between agencies and courts that has resulted in an even more blurred line between law and equity, which further harms the common law system.

Section IV A: Exhaustion Rule

The exhaustion rule is composed of two general rules: (1) the exhaustion rule says all administrative remedies must be exhausted, and (2) primary jurisdiction, which says that if the primary jurisdiction is that of an administrative agency then the case must first be taken there, and all remedies must be exhausted before the court can hear the case. The two rules amount to generally the same thing, which is administrative remedies must be exhausted where such agencies have jurisdiction, before the case can be heard in court. These two rules combined are commonly referred to as the exhaustion rule. The first part of the exhaustion rule is well established; in 1969, the Supreme Court said in *McKart v. United States*[45] that

> the doctrine of exhaustion of administrative remedies is well established in the jurisprudence of administrative law. . . . Courts ordinarily should not interfere with an agency until it has completed its action, or else has clearly exceeded its jurisdiction. (395 U.S. 193, 194, 1969)[46]

The exhaustion rule was so strong at one point that it even overpowered Congress's authority to invoke the Commerce Clause in front of the Supreme Court. In *Illinois Commerce Commission v. Thomson*[47] the Court said, "injunction against railroad rate order should have been denied because of failure first to pursue the administrative remedy" (318 U.S. 686, 1943). The decision in *Illinois Commerce Commission* was based on a precedent established in 1938 by *Myers v. Bethlehem Shipbuilding Corp.*[48] that said a "long settled rule of judicial administration that no one is entitled to judicial relief for a supposed or threatened injury until the prescribed administrative remedy has been exhausted" (303 U.S. 51, 1938).

Primary jurisdiction was a little less clear since the jurisdictional boundaries were not always codified, and when new cases arose, there may not have been a clear controlling precedent in order to determine primary jurisdiction. In most decisions where the Supreme Court has granted primary jurisdiction to an administrative agency, the claim dealt with commerce and economic issues. In *Ricci v. Chicago Mercantile Exchange*[49] the Court decided that a defendant who had allegedly violated both antitrust laws and the Commodity Exchange Act must first face administrative hearings by the Commodity Exchange Commission before it could make a decision on the antitrust violations. Similar decisions were reached in both *United States v. Western Pacific Railroad*[50] and *Arrow Transportation Company v. S. Ry.*[51] In these cases the Court decided that it would refuse any action sought until a decision had been made by the Interstate Commerce Commission. In cases that do not deal with economic matters, the Court is much more likely to invoke its own jurisdiction as will be discussed below, and in Section IV B.

Raoul Berger writes, "from the beginning, the exhaustion rule was formulated in terms of equity jurisdiction" (Berger 1939, 981). The Court soon found, in its application of the exhaustion rule, that the precedents which governed the relationship between law and equity would not produce the right results if applied directly to the relationship between courts and agencies (Laycock 1991, 136) The exhaustion rule applies to both law and equity. In *Myers* the Court said that "because the rule is one of judicial administration —not merely a rule governing the exercise of discretion—it is applicable to proceedings at law as well as suits in equity" (303 U.S. 51, 1938). *McGee v. United States*[52] shows just how blurred the lines can become. In *McGee* the court barred the defendant a defense from criminal prosecution because he had not exhausted all administrative remedies. So even when the case is not in equity, the Court may still give the administrative agency primary jurisdiction, and thus allow a case of law to be heard by an agency, potentially violating the defendant's right to due process. The Court has also decided that when a plaintiff seeks damages against an administrative agency, and precedent would award damages to the plaintiff, the Court concedes primary jurisdiction to the agency against which the damages are sought as in *First National Bank v. Board of County Commissioners*,[53] when the Court dismissed the case for a tax refund because the plaintiff failed to exhaust administrative remedies. In *First National Bank* the Court had the authority to hear the case under its legal jurisdiction as there was a legal remedy, but in making it a suit in equity, it was able to hand it off to an administrative agency. Thus, the rules that usually govern law and equity do not always apply to the relationship between agencies and courts. The irreparable injury rule, as established through precedent, said that all legal remedies had to be exhausted before equity relief could be sought. But when making decisions on primary jurisdiction the Court does not require that legal remedies be exhausted before equitable remedies are pursued, even if the plaintiff is only seeking a legal remedy. This last part is of particular importance. Under a common law system, the decision to file a suit in law or to seek equitable relief was made by the plaintiff prior to the trial. Under new practice, the Court is able to make the decision of how the suit ought to be filed after the trial has begun but before handing down its verdict. The decision on how the suit will be filed ultimately rests in the hands of a judge. Finally, when a legal remedy is sought by a plaintiff, the Court acts as if it were free to place the suit in equity and not address the legal issues even if the plaintiff does not seek equitable relief. This is similar to what occurs when the court invokes immunity on behalf of judges, legislators, and the president.

Section IV B: Exceptions to the Exhaustion Rule

There are four general standards that the courts apply in deciding whether an exception can be granted to the exhaustion rule: (1) issues of law, (2) constitutional challenges, (3) challenges to the agency's jurisdiction, and (4) cases when the agency cannot provide adequate relief. What follows will be an examination of cases where the Supreme Court has granted exceptions under these standards. I will show that these standards are susceptible to manipulation by the Court in that they are not definitive standards and are commonly violated.

In *McKart* the Court says that the issue of administrative remedies is a well-established issue, but this decision is an example of when the Court violates said well-established issue. *McKart* says that in issues of statutory interpretation that require neither expertise nor discretion, and when it is too late to exhaust administrative remedies, the Court will be able to invoke its own jurisdiction. What is interesting is the pattern of citations used by the majority in *McKart*. It liberally cites cases that have established the issue of administrative remedies, but does not find a single case to support its opinion that there should be exceptions to this rule. This does seem peculiar since one would expect that if the Court were going to challenge a long-established issue it would want to ground its decision to do so in some other area of precedent. And while *McKart* is not the first case to employ exceptions to the exhaustion rule it is certainly one of the more interesting cases since it so openly argues for how well established the exhaustion rule is, and then makes a decision which goes against this rule.

The Supreme Court assumes the role of being the final arbiter of constitutional matters; thus it is not surprising that it will exercise its jurisdiction when there exists a constitutional matter to be settled by an administrative agency. One reason is that the Court does not think that an administrative agency will give a constitutional issue its due respect. In *Mathews v. Eldridge*[54] the Court stated in its opinion that "it is unrealistic to expect that the Secretary would consider substantial changes in the current administrative review system at the behest of a single aid recipient raising a constitutional challenge in an adjudicatory context" (422 U.S. 767, 1975). *Mathews* sets the precedent that the Court may not only exert jurisdiction over constitutional matters, but may, if it chooses to, revise an agency's practices it deems inconsistent with constitutional principles. Even when the issue deals with the eligibility for Social Security benefits, the Court has found a way to make it a constitutional matter, and thus exert its jurisdiction. In *Weinberger v. Salfi*[55] the majority on the Court wrote that when a challenge to a social security statute is raised it may be considered a constitutional challenge, and such a challenge is beyond the competence of the agency; thus raising such a challenge to the agency is "futile and wasteful." The Supreme Court upheld a decision made by the California Superior Court which stated, "it would be heroic indeed to compel a party to appear before an administrative body to challenge its very existence and to expect a dispassionate hearing . . . on the constitutionality of the statute establishing its status and functions" (12 California 3d 237). This reasoning seems ironic considering that the federal judiciary has upheld its right to interpret the constitutionality of the various Judiciary Acts that establish its status and functions. So while the Court is able to make unbiased decisions when its status is being challenged, as in immunity cases, other agencies cannot act in such a dispassionate manner and must turn jurisdiction over to the courts.

A powerful tool in the Court's arsenal is its ability to define the jurisdiction of an administrative agency. While the second half of the exhaustion rule requires that the administrative agency hears the case if it has primary jurisdiction, the Court has shown its power to define an agency's jurisdiction, thus voiding this portion of the exhaustion rule. In *Public Utility Commission v. United States*[56] the Court decided that it had jurisdiction over the case because the litigant was constitutionally immune from the agency's jurisdiction, even though the agency in question was given statutory jurisdiction. Kenneth Culp Davis analyzed fourteen Supreme Court cases made on this issue and he found that only half required exhaustion and those that did not require exhaustion did not because the Court decided that the agency did not have jurisdiction (Davis 1958). The Supreme Court is not the only court to limit the scope of the exhaustion rule. Illinois' highest court handed down a decision which was subsequently upheld by the Supreme Court. *Landfill, Inc. v. Pollution Control Board*[57] stated that exhaustion is not required "where an administrative body's assertion of jurisdiction is attacked on its face and in its entirety on the ground that it is not authorized by statute" (74 Illinois 2d. 551, 1978). This establishes an interesting precedent. So long as an agency's jurisdiction is challenged it loses its jurisdiction to the court. If a litigant wished to enjoin a court and leave the jurisdiction of an agency, it need only challenge the statutory basis of its jurisdiction. While this does not guarantee being heard by a court, one certainly can make the argument that precedent establishes the right to do so.

The issue of the inadequacy of agency relief is a two-fold problem. One, it allows the court to decide on a matter of adequacy that it may not have jurisdiction to. Two, it complicates the matter of law and equity. Since the ability of an agency to offer relief is based on statute, the court's denial that this statute offers an adequate remedy says that statutory remedy is less adequate in that situation than the equitable remedy which only the court is able to provide. At the end of Section IV A I demonstrated how the courts have been able to make the switch from law to equity in order to get a decision into the jurisdiction of an agency, and now I show that the courts are able to make the same switch to get the case into its own jurisdiction. In *Myers v. Caple*[58] the administrative remedy was found to be inadequate and therefore exhaustion was not required. How is the remedy found to be inadequate if the available remedies were not exhausted? In *Moore v. Pacific Northwest Bell* and *Foree v. Crown Cent. Petroleum Corp.* the decisions handed down said that the agencies did not have the ability or authority to grant the remedy sought. The remedies sought were filed in equity, and a legal remedy was available that had been established as adequate before by the Supreme Court. Not only did the decisions say that the statutory remedies were incapable of providing adequate relief, but the agencies were denied jurisdiction in equity. Furthermore, the Court failed to apply the irreparable injury rule. They simply said that an equitable remedy was sought and thus should be granted before deciding if the law provided an adequate remedy. This shows a mighty inconsistency in the judiciary's decision to grant equitable relief when these decisions are contrasted with those that cite the irreparable injury rule as the basis for deciding when equitable relief should be granted.

CONCLUSION

This chapter began with an unsettled debate, and has ended with some ideas about who was correct in that debate. I do not presume to have settled the issues that were discussed during the time of ratification; however, the preceding review of Supreme Court cases gives some insight into whose vision of the judiciary was more accurate: the Federalists' or the Anti-Federalists'. What the preceding review shows is that there has been an inconsistency in the Court's application of equity jurisdiction. The inconsistency has generated a distorted line of separation between law and equity. This distortion has led to increased authority in the hands of the federal government in general, and specifically in the hands of the federal judiciary. The Court has been able to maneuver in the same way that the Anti-Federalists said it would. It has been able to switch from law to equity when convenient, and to interpret the Constitution and statutory laws based on their intent and not their written word. I must say that I have not proven that the Anti-Federalists were correct; that would require a more extensive examination into the effects of Supreme Court decisions on the other branches, independent government agencies, and the public's perception of the national government. All that is necessary for this chapter is that I show how the Court is able to define and redefine its own jurisdiction without regard for standing precedents, statutory laws, or other constitutional restraints.

Let it be recognized as well that the effects of a deteriorating common law system has been encouraged by an unrestricted system of equity decisions. Surbin concludes his article by writing:

> Over the years, those who have both stressed individual rights and liberties, and distrusted centralized power, have also criticized unbridled equity power. Maitland and others warned that although equity and law worked well complementing each other, equity without common law had the capacity to be unwieldy and chaotic. (Surbin 1987, 1001)

Combining the effects the Court's use of equity jurisdiction and the findings from the previous two chapters, we may conclude that the essential elements of the common law system have been eroded, primarily through the actions and innovations brought forth by the legal community. The deterioration of the common law system is not an inherently negative development, and had it been replaced with a system that provided for an even greater amount of community involvement and restraint on arbitrary government action, then perhaps it would have been a positive development. What has been witnessed, however, is the deterioration of the common law system, which has resulted in an increasingly powerful judiciary and an infringement on state sovereignty which amounts to fewer restrictions on arbitrary government action.

NOTES

1. All references to *The Federalist Papers* are to the Carey and McClellan (2001) edition. In some sense it seems as if Hamilton and Brutus are on the same page in that Brutus does not say that the Constitution "directly empowers" the courts to do so, only that it is implied, or through possible implication. Hamilton does not deny the possibility.
2. If our understanding of common law given in chapter 2 is correct, then this formulation is backward, it would seem.
3. More time will be spent discussing the relationship between the Supreme Court and Congress in Section IV of this chapter.
4. One of the differences between the Federalists and Anti-Federalists is that the Anti-Federalists focused on what could happen and the Federalists tended to disagree by saying the conclusions their opponents drew were unlikely.
5. 328 U.S. 395 (1946).
6. 347 U.S. 483 (1954) and 349 U.S. 294 (1955).
7. 403 U.S. 388 (1971).
8. 532 U.S. 275 (2001).
9. A striking difference between the two cases is that *Bivens* deals with an individual and *Alexander* deals with a government agency. The court seemingly says that individuals within the government may be held responsible by providing a financial remedy, but not government agencies.
10. 446 U.S. 14 (1980).

11. 462 U.S. 367 (1983), 487 U.S. 412 (1988), 462 U.S. 296 (1983), 483 U.S. 669 (1987), 510 U.S. 471 (1994), and 112 S. Ct. 515 (2001).

12. 22 U.S. (9 Wheat.) 738 (1824).

13. Legislation was also passed in the wake of *Bivens* to provide statutory support for the decision. These two examples of congressional action as a direct result of, and in accord with, judicial decisions brings some doubt to the thesis found in Gerald Rosenberg's *Hollow Hope*.

14. A more extensive discussion of the protection received by the federal government will take place in Section III.

15. 684 S. W.2d. 592, 595 (Mo. App. 1985).

16. Douglas Laycock (1991) lists each of these cases, 35–36, fn. 80–81.

17. 508 U.S. 248 (1993).

18. 415 U.S. 651 (1974).

19. While it may not be found in text of the Constitution, let the reader not forget that Hamilton gave validity to the idea in *Federalist* 81 when he wrote, "it is inherent in the nature of the sovereignty not to be amenable to the suit of an individual without its consent."

20. 435 U.S. 349 (1978).

21. 764 F. 2d 294 (5th Cir. 1986).

22. *Martinez v. Winner* 771 F. 2d 424, 432–35 (10th Cir. 1985).

23. 994 F.2d 1121 (5th Cir. 1993).

24. 502 U.S. 9 (1992).

25. 460 U.S. 325 (1983).

26. 28 F. 3d 1249 (D.C. Cir. 1994).

27. 19 F. 3d 552 (11th Cir. 1994).

28. *Antoine v. Byers and Anderson, Inc.*, 508 U.S. 429 (1993).

29. *Zarcone v Perry*, 572 F. 2d 52 (2nd Cir. 1978) and *Maestri v. Jutkofsky*, 860 F. 2d 50 (2nd Cir. 1988).

30. 421 U.S. 491 (1975).

31. 408 U.S. 606 (1972).

32. 408 U.S. 501 (1972).

33. 457 U.S. 731 (1982).

34. 418 U.S. 683 (1974).

35. This section has shown that when judges face criminal charges they are granted immunity.

36. 520 U.S. 681 (1997).

37. Notice how much more limited presidential immunity is in this case than for judges as discussed in *Malina*. Furthermore, it should not be lost on the reader that this decision was made against a Democratic president by a decidedly conservative court.

38. 2 U.S. (2 Dall.) 419.

39. 440 U.S. 410 (1979).

40. 209 U.S. 123 (1908).

41. 239 U.S. 33 (1915).

42. *Ex Parte Young* finds its precedent in *Smyth v. Ames*, 169 U.S. 466 (1898). A more complete analysis of the role the Fourteenth Amendment has played in the application of the Eleventh Amendment is William Fletcher's "A Historical Interpretation of the Eleventh Amendment: A Narrow Construction of an Affirmative Grant of Jurisdiction Rather than a Prohibition Against Jurisdiction," *Stanford Law Review* 1033 (1983).

43. 465 U.S. 89 (1984). The Appellate decision enjoined the agency with the state as the state law had directed, but the Supreme Court overruled this decision and directed that state law be ignored and the agency and the state should not be enjoined.

44. *Atascadero State Hospital v. Scanlon*, 473 U.S. 234 (1985) and *Dellmuth v. Muth*, 491 U.S. 223 (1989).

45. 395 U.S. 185 (1969).

46. Section IV B highlights the inconsistency in the reasoning of this opinion.

47. 318 U.S. 675 (1943).

48. 303 U.S. 41 (1938).

49. 409 U.S. 289 (1973).

50. 352 U.S. 59 (1956).

51. 372 U.S. 658 (1963).

52. 402 U.S. 479 (1971).

53. 264 U.S. 450 (1924).

54. 422 U.S. 749 (1975).

55. 422 U.S. 749 (1975).

56. 355 U.S. 534 (1958).

57. 74 Illinois 2d. 541 (1978).

58. 258 N.W. 2d. 301 (Iowa 1977).

6

Montesquieu as the Intellectual Forerunner

This chapter will make explicit the argument supported by the findings in chapters 3–5. The system argued for by Alexander Hamilton is the one which has developed. This is a system which tends toward centralization with the judiciary playing a vital role in the move toward a more national system. This chapter will show that this has occurred not by chance, but was part of the plan of Alexander Hamilton. In order to make this point clear, I must take the scenic route. Beginning with Charles de Secondat Baron de Montesquieu and moving to William Blackstone, it will be shown that the American system was the result of something more than a peculiar set of circumstances that joined together to get us where we are today. First I will give an account of Montesquieu's interpretation of history. It will be shown that Montesquieu's view of history led to his determination that human intervention was necessary to prevent the unpredictability that is associated with historical progression. Montesquieu's presentation of history reveals history's tendency to bring about moderation, a process which Montesquieu seeks to replicate through institutional design.[1] Within the institutional design there is an instrument which serves as the moderating force. This instrument is not simply a separation of powers, but it is nested within that system.

Next I will move on to William Blackstone. This section will show how Blackstone mimicked the thinking of Montesquieu in a number of important ways, but primarily in how he envisioned the judiciary and the need for the proper sort of men to be involved in the governing process in order to protect against the capriciousness which was possible when proper guidance was absent. Before I attempt an exegesis of Blackstone's judiciary and its role in the governing process I will give an account of Blackstone's view of history and show how it too follows the thought of Montesquieu. Throughout the discussion on Blackstone, it will be shown that Blackstone's use of the judiciary and law are quite similar to Montesquieu's but departures do occur, and the departures occur because Blackstone takes Montesquieu's principles and lessons to the next logical step. While Montesquieu laid the groundwork for Blackstone, he did not restrain Blackstone from making his own insights.

Finally I move on to Alexander Hamilton. This section draws the same parallels that were drawn in the previous section. I will show that the thought of Hamilton is the result of taking Montesquieu's view of history to an extreme. Hamilton understands history for its lessons, but that which has occurred need not be replicated but replaced by a new system of government because the earlier systems have failed. Thus, it is through human innovation that the progression of human activity will occur, not history. Hamilton says that history ought to be controlled, if not abandoned, in favor of a more rational system. This requires an energetic and centralized system of governing that is guided by a moderating force. Hamilton gives man the authority to control the forces of history, whereas Montesquieu says we must respect history's influence when developing governments and laws as history shapes the character of the people. Hamilton, on the other hand, has much less respect for history's influence on human character and much more confidence in the power to impose law and government on the people. The gulf between Hamilton and Montesquieu is bridged by Blackstone, who makes the transition from a judiciary who can gradually and unobtrusively implement reform, to a judiciary who can create positive law. The last question, then, is whether Hamilton misapplied the thought of Montesquieu and Blackstone, or if he merely extended their principles to a degree which they did not.

SECTION I: MONTESQUIEU

Montesquieu's teaching is based on the lessons of history. His understanding of history is the basis for his political philosophy and the way he transmits that philosophy. In Montesquieu we see an effort to derive political standards from history. "It is in the thought of Montesquieu that the need to derive some moral and political standards from history, history understood as opposed to, or as the replacement for nature, comes into the foreground of the tradition of political philosophy" (Pangle 1973, 9).[2] The lesson of history is moderation. History resolves itself by balancing extremes and achieving moderation, and it is the moderate resolutions that are desired by Montesquieu. This is the historical dialectic as Montesquieu understands it.[3] Montesquieu presents history to us in such a way that we see that history achieves moderation by destroying those nations that lie in the extremes. Athens and Marseilles were destroyed when they abandoned their moderate base. When Rome became an empire it too was destroyed as a result of abandoning its moderate principles of republicanism. This reading of history leads Montesquieu to conclude that the proper political order is the order which is moderate. Before a consideration of Montesquieu's political philosophy commences, we must understand his history, as it is the teaching of Montesquieu that demands this approach.[4]

Montesquieu substitutes history for nature. It was the tradition of the liberal theorists before him, specifically Hobbes and Locke, to give an account of human nature as the basis of their political philosophy. Montesquieu does not follow their lead, but instead builds on another foundation, a foundation based on history and laws, since "Nature always acts, but it is overwhelmed by social customs."[5] For Montesquieu it is the laws and history which dictate human nature, not the other way around. In Book V.3 Montesquieu says

> The good sense and happiness of individuals largely consists in their having middling talents and fortunes. If a republic whose *laws have formed many middling people* is composed of sober people, it will be governed soberly; if it is composed of happy people, it will be very happy. (Book V.3, italics my own)[6]

Montesquieu draws these conclusions from his reading of history, and transmits these lessons to the reader by providing historical examples in such a way that shows the different defects of each system and how the defects could have been corrected had the nations better understood the effects of custom, tradition, and history; and Montesquieu then shows how failed nations might have directed the effects of custom, tradition, and history through the proper implementation of laws.[7] A nice example of this is how he shows that the effects of wealth are not the same in all circumstances. While wealth worked wonderfully in modern England, it led to destruction in both Carthage and Rome. In the following subsections I will develop this point by analyzing Montesquieu's treatment of Athens, Marseilles, and Saint Louis IX.

Section I A: Athens and Marseilles

The dialectic progression of history must be derived from his use of historical examples, as he does not make an explicit statement about his view of history.[8] When he describes Athens in Book V, Montesquieu draws the reader's attention more to the internal conflict taking place within Athens than he does to the external war with Sparta. Athens, as with all commercial republics, must find the balance between anarchy and republicanism. The evil effects of commerce—inequality, selfishness, physical growth—can be balanced by the positive effects of commerce—"frugality, economy, moderation, work, prudence, tranquility, order, and rule" (Book V.6)—if the people and government are prudent. It was the fate of Athens to fall as it had not properly balanced the positive and negative benefits of a commercial republic, which resulted in corruption from within. Within Athens it was not the fault of the leaders, but the people who "applied themselves more to eloquence than to military arts" (Book VIII.2). The people of Athens had turned lazy and inequality resulted from their commercial success, despite the best efforts of Solon to reform the laws in such a way that would encourage equality. Inequality led to greed, laziness, and excess. Contrast this with Sparta, whose prudence was captured by Montesquieu in his citation of Plato: "'We offer common things,' said a Spartan, 'so that we have the means for honoring the gods every day'" (Book XXV.7). Internal unrest in Athens did not begin with its domestic policies, but with its foreign agenda. As a commercial republic Athens was not built to be a military empire; its expansion would have to be due to its commercial success if it was to be successful. One of the responsibilities of the laws in a republic is to keep the people humble, and the people cannot remain humble if their nation's success is attributed to their involvement.

Great successes, especially those to which the people contribute much, make them so arrogant that it is no longer possible to guide them. Jealous of the magistrates, they become jealous of the magistracy; enemies of those who govern, they soon become enemies of the constitution. In this way the victory at Salamis over the Persians corrupted the republic of Athens; in this way the defeat of the Athenians ruined the republic of Syracuse (Book VIII.4).

Athens fell because it was unable to balance its ambition for external greatness with the need for domestic tranquility. The laws of Athens were unable to produce a people that were consistent with the requirements of a republican government. Athens was unable, perhaps unwilling, to recognize and support its true spirit through its laws. It failed to recognize the "spirit of the laws."

Montesquieu balances the picture he paints of Athens with that of ancient Marseilles. In Athens, their success bred jealousy, and this jealousy contributed to its downfall, as jealousy runs counter to the positive effects of commerce. "Jealous of the magistrates, they become jealous of the magistracy; enemies of those who govern, they soon become enemies of the constitution" (Book VIII.4). In some sense it was the greatness of Athens that led to its downfall, and Marseilles then was protected from the same fate, since "The republic of Marseilles never underwent these great shifts from lowliness to greatness; thus, it always governed itself with wisdom; thus, it preserved its principles" (Book VIII.4). Marseilles is an example of a commercial republic which was able to balance its competing forces in order to endure.

Marseilles, during its high point, was moderate. Montesquieu acknowledges that the general purpose of each state is to preserve itself, each state having a purpose peculiar to it, which in the case of Marseilles was the preservation of public tranquility (Book XI.5). Like all nations, Marseilles is restrained by factors its nation cannot control, such as climate and geography. But what a nation can control is how it reacts to the uncontrollable elements, and a government that reacts correctly to its environment will be able to preserve itself.

Marseilles, a necessary retreat in the midst of a stormy sea, Marseilles, where all the winds, the shoals, and the coastline order ships to put in, was frequented by seafaring people. The barrenness of its territory made its citizens decide on economic commerce. They had to be hardworking in order to replace that which nature refused them; just, in order to live among the barbarian nations that were to make their prosperity; moderate, in order for their government always to be tranquil; finally, of frugal mores, in order to live always by a commerce that would the more surely preserve the less it was advantageous to them (Book XX.5).

But like Athens, Marseilles fell, and fell because of internal strife, a civil war that was the result of an inadequate constitution and governing system that could not prevent the citizens from becoming lazy and being overtaken by the Gauls and civil war. It was the inability to establish a balance between industry and power. Marseilles chose to focus its attention and resources internally by being a commercial giant which would bring it riches. It did not balance the need to be a force in foreign affairs with its desire for domestic tranquility. Marseilles, like Athens, did not recognize the proper character of its government or people, or in Montesquieu's terms, it did not adhere to the "spirit of the laws." Placing these two governments side by side, one can see the dialectic between Athens and Marseilles develop. If one were to match the negative features of one with the positive features of the other, one would have a properly balanced commercial republic. Such a state would exhibit moderation as a result of the interaction between ambition and priorities.

The examples of Athens and Marseilles show that when a state moves to the extreme, and ignores its history, it loses stability. As time progresses, states exhibit less movement toward the extremes and more toward moderation, which is what we see when we compare Montesquieu's treatment of Athens and Marseilles. Montesquieu uses history to show that the progression of history leads to more moderate regimes by simply eliminating those that are not moderate. This is not to say that history affects all nations in the same way, or all progress at the same rate, but it does say that the states which endure do so because of their moderation. This point is reinforced in his presentation of Saint Louis IX, who was able to balance the extreme forces of liberty with the extreme forces of stability when he combined Germanic and Roman law.

Section I B: Saint Louis IX

The reader's attention is drawn to Book XXVIII when he notices that it is the longest of all the books. Book XXVIII discusses Saint Louis in the most detail. The historical dialectic can be seen taking shape under the rule of a single king. Such is the case with Saint Louis IX, under whose leadership two extreme historical forces came together. Saint Louis took over a state in shambles; the rule of law was unclear, as too was the future of the state and the path it would take. The Germanic laws were the laws of the people who settled France and by extension the basis of French laws, especially its civil procedure. The church canon law and Roman law[9] were threats to the German law. French law was not directly controlled by the clergy as it was in Spain, but the influence was felt in the method of pleading. The French courts adopted the practice of defending oneself by swearing an evangelical oath, against which there was no recourse in civil law, save for a test of endurance. The test of endurance rested on such things as combat or withstanding the burns from fire or boiling water. Such tests proved the authenticity of the defendant's claims as it would be only through God's power that they would be able to withstand the tests of endurance, and God would only support those whose oaths were truthful. This system is quite a distance from German procedure that had such safeguards as trial by jury and an adversarial system of law.

When his reign began, Louis instituted reforms—reforms that would bring stability and liberty to the system through balance and moderation. The success of Louis' reforms was due to the gradual manner in which they were implemented. He did not eliminate the traditions and customs that already existed; instead he implemented new laws that would gently guide the traditions and customs. He integrated the new provisions with the old customs. Saint Louis took to making reforms through a trial-and-error approach. While he maintained a view of the big picture, he was not constrained by a single pedagogy. Montesquieu praises Saint Louis for the method he chose to institute his reforms.

> The code we have under the name of the *Establishments* of Saint Louis was never made to serve as law for the whole kingdom. . . . Now, at a time when each town, borough, or village had its own custom, to give a general body of civil laws was to want to reverse in a moment all the particular laws under which men had lived everywhere in the kingdom. To make a general custom of all the particular customs would be rash, even in these times when princes find only obedience everywhere . . . one surely sees that to undertake to change the accepted laws and usages everywhere was something that could not enter the minds of those who governed. (Book XXVIII.37)

And in case there was any doubt remaining about the method Saint Louis adopted, Montesquieu reports:

> When one saw in his tribunals, and in those of the lords, a more natural, more reasonable way of proceeding, a way more in conformity with morality, religion, public tranquility, and the security of persons and goods, it was taken up and the other was abandoned.
>
> To invite when one must not constrain, to lead when one must not command, is the supreme skill. Reason has a natural empire; it has even a tyrannical empire: one resists it, but this resistance is its triumph; yet a little time and one is forced to come back to it. (Book XVIII.38)

The method and target of Louis' reforms is the model for a prudent legislator who could implant reason and moderation in the laws. His method was subtle and gradual; "so that the change would be felt less," Saint Louis "removed the thing and let the terms continue to exist" (Book XXVIII.29). As Paul O. Carrese notes, "The very spirit of Montesquieu's political philosophy animates these extraordinary pronouncements." (Carrese 2003, 260) The process was dialectic. Louis was successful, and held in such high regard by Montesquieu, for following the natural dialectic of things, best exhibited in history, and now in good rulers. However, it was the randomness of history that brought Louis to power, not the design of the system. There was no conscious effort, or foresight, to select a king who would create a moderate system through gradual reform. The regime could have easily brought another ruler to power who would not have been as praiseworthy, and that is what Montesquieu wants to prevent through his teaching. Montesquieu wants to ensure, through institutional means, that the government in place is moderate and brings about reforms gradually.

The most notable triumph of Saint Louis was the reform of the French legal system. He replaced the tradition of trial by combat by combining Roman law with local customary law. Trial by combat was based on ancient Frankish law, which had its origins in the barbarian tribes. Saint Louis learned of the Roman law with the newly recovered Institutes of Justinian (Book XXVIII.42). Saint Louis was able to accomplish something through moderate reform that the Romans were unable to do by force, which was to institute Roman law in a land that was dominated by local custom and barbaric laws, while still preserving the spirit of the people.[10] One of his methods for injecting Roman law was so subtle that it could hardly be considered a reform. In order to persuade the men of the law he had the Roman laws translated so that they could be better understood by these men; it was through this process that there grew distaste for French law, which was replaced by an affinity for Roman law (Book XXVIII.38). The result was that the men who practiced and made the laws would perpetuate the reforms gradually as they unobtrusively influenced others. "There was an internal vice in this compilation: it formed an amphibious code, in which were mixed French jurisprudence and Roman law; things were brought together that had never been related and that were often contradictory" (Book XXVIII.38). Conjoining these two systems was a positive accomplishment, as vice is used here to bring about a sense of something desirable.[11]

The negative effects of Roman law were felt soon after the reign of Louis IX ended. However, Montesquieu points out that it was not the result of Louis IX, but the fault of those who followed.

> The judicial forms introduced by Saint Louis ceased to be used. This prince had in view less the thing itself, that is, the best way of judging, than the best way of replacing the former practice of judging. The first object was to evoke a dislike for the old jurisprudence, and the second to form a new one. But once the drawbacks of the new one had appeared, another was soon seen to supplant it.[12] (Book XXVIII.39)

The failure of Louis' successors was that they did not supplant a new law when the drawbacks became apparent with the application of Roman law.

The historical dialectic is readily observable in Montesquieu's treatment of France, the ebb and flow between Germanic law and Roman law, Frankish law and church law, serves as the analysis for Book XXVIII. The aim of Book XXVIII is to draw the reader's attention to the balancing tendency of opposing forces when applied correctly, and the necessity of these opposing forces being present in order to achieve moderation. The success of Saint Louis ended when the adopted Roman law was allowed to proceed unconstrained. The Roman law that was adopted was the law of the Roman Empire, not the Roman Republic. This law limited the number of safeguards that were present in the French jurisprudence that had been adopted from the German tribes, whose goal was always to promote liberty.[13] What made Saint Louis successful was his recognition of the need to balance liberty with stability, which is why he integrated both Gothic and Roman law. But if stability is not balanced with liberty, then a system of restraint takes over at the cost of liberty.[14] This is what happened when Saint Louis was out of power. What resulted was a system in France that was without tribunals of one's peers, a system of appeals, and decisions that conformed to popular judgments. Instead, French jurisprudence turned into a system "which was employed everywhere . . . to regulate, limit, correct, and extend French jurisprudence" (Book XXVIII.38). The adoption of Roman law led to a deterioration of both ancient Frankish law and customary practices.

> When Roman right was translated, when it began to be taught in the schools . . . peers and chivalrous men were no longer in a position to judge; peers began to withdraw from the tribunals of the lord . . . the more so because judgments . . . had become only a practice that they neither knew nor wanted to know. (Book XXVIII.42)

The tendency of the Roman law was toward centralization and uniformity of the law. A *parlement* appointed by the king was to be the court of final appeal and supervise the court system.

> The *parlement* judged in the last resort on almost all the business of the kingdom. It had formerly judged only those between dukes, counts, bishops, abbots, or between the king and his vassals in their relation to the political order. Later, one was obliged to make it a sitting *parlement* and keep it permanently assembled. . . . Scarcely had the *parlement* become a fixed body than one began to compile its decisions (Book XXVIII.39). . . . The *parlement*, which had taken, for its form of procedure, everything good and useful from that of the clerical tribunals, soon saw only its abuses; and, as royal jurisdiction became stronger daily, it was increasingly in a position to correct for these same abuses. Indeed, they were intolerable. (Book XXVIII.41)

In discussing the devastating effects of the Roman law after Louis' reign, Montesquieu also forces the reader to notice that the history of the people must always be respected. No law or reform can challenge the customs and traditions too overtly without creating disorder. Louis was successful not because of the reforms he chose necessarily, but because of the reform method he chose. This is a lesson to be learned from Montesquieu's discussion of how Roman law became oppressive after Louis' reign.

The English Constitution provided the proper balance through its conjoining of custom, Gothic law, Roman law, and commerce. The English constitution protected liberty by respecting custom, provided stability through its adoption of Roman law, the threat of centralization brought by Roman law was combated by the atomization tendency of commerce, and the opposing forces of Gothic and Roman law balanced one another, under the English constitution, and established a structure for moderate reform.[15] The historical dialectic was institutionalized in England, and dare we say, the English constitution represents the end of history for Montesquieu?[16] This treatment of history shows that if forces are understood scientifically they are not beyond human control. As Shklar (1986) points out, "To know physical nature is to be able to control it intelligently. . . . A scientific jurisprudence must know even more: it must understand the character of the lawmakers" (Shklar 1986, 93). Since power is inimical to moderate human character, human character must be controlled by laws and institutions in the form of a constitution, and the best constitution is found in England, where interests and powers check one another.

> In order to form a moderate government, one must combine powers, regulate them, temper them, make them act; one must give one power a ballast, so to speak, to put it in a position to resist another; *this is a masterpiece of legislation that chance rarely produces and prudence is rarely allowed to produce*. (Book V.14, italics my own)

Section I C: The English Constitution

Montesquieu's discussion of the origins of English law follows the same pattern that he uses in developing the origins of French law, the pattern which is unveiled in the above discussion of Louis IX. The importance of the Gothic influence on French law discussed throughout Book XXVIII is reinforced by the discussion of the Gothic influence on English law in Book XI. Toward the end of the sixth chapter in Book XI Montesquieu paraphrases Tacitus and says, "one will see that the English have taken their idea of political government from the Germans"(XI.6). The English constitution had liberty as its end, just as Gothic law did. The English constitution created a system of separation of powers which separated the judiciary from executive and legislative control, and control of the legislature was left in the hands of the representatives, not the people (Books XI.6 and 11, VIII.6).[17] After a discussion of Montesquieu's separation of powers principle and the central role of the judiciary within that system, I will turn to a discussion of how this system alleviates the problems of past republics and brings history under the control of men. It is not necessary to give a detailed review of how Montesquieu sees the English constitution working; all that I need to show are the reasons why he favors this system, and why the nucleus of the system is in the hands of judges.

Section I C.1: Separation of Powers

Separating the three powers of government from one another is a way of constructing a government that will not violate the liberty of its citizens. Montesquieu's political science is an attempt at creating a moderate system by balancing competing forces. (Book V.14)

This statement occurs well before the explicit discussion of the English constitution in Books XI and XII, but foreshadows the teaching in those books that says the proper government is one that has proper balance which leads to moderate policies. Montesquieu also foreshadows his argument in Books XI and XII that something more than legislation is necessary to bring this sort of government about; in addition to proper legislation it requires a constitution, a proper form of government, and an acknowledgement of the nation's customs and history. What is interesting from this list is what is missing: Montesquieu does not rely on virtue as did the ancient republics, nor does he rely on the spirit of patriotism as the earlier republics did; instead he relies on man's ability to create institutions which will bring about results that were only thought possible when great men were in control. This sentiment is captured in Book XI when he writes:

> Even virtue has need of limits. So that one cannot abuse power, power must check power by the arrangement of things. A constitution can be such that no one will be constrained to do the things the law does not oblige him to do or be kept from doing the things the law permits him to do. (Book XI.4)

When this paragraph is paired with the excerpt from Book V, Montesquieu's intention becomes clear. Liberty is the proper end of government, it is through moderation that liberty can be achieved, and moderation can be realized if the government is properly constructed.[18] Thus, one sees a break from the ancients in Montesquieu as he gives up the search and demand for a philosopher-king.[19]

Montesquieu spends so much time on England since "There is also one nation in the world whose constitution has political liberty for its direct purpose" (Book XI.5). Montesquieu makes an effort to draw a distinction between the England that exists, and the one he is studying. When referring to England's constitution he clearly is not addressing the results of its constitution, but instead to what ought to come about as a result of a constitution with liberty as its end. "It is not for me to examine whether at present the English enjoy this liberty or not. It suffices for me to say that it is established by their laws, and I seek no further" (Book XI.6). In either case, it is clear what Montesquieu defines as liberty.

> It is true in democracies the people seem to do what they want, but political liberty in no way consists in doing what one wants. . . . Liberty is the right to do everything the laws permit; and if one citizen could do what they forbid, he would no longer have liberty because the others would likewise have this same power (XI.3). . . . Political liberty in a citizen is that tranquility of spirit which comes from the opinion each one has of his security; and in order for him to have this liberty, the government must be such that one citizen cannot fear another citizen. (Book XI.6)

And according to Montesquieu, "Political liberty is found only in moderate governments" (Book XI.6). This is what leads Montesquieu to the idea of abandoning the philosopher-king model and seeking a new political science on which he can base a system which balances power, since political liberty "is present only when power is not abused, but it has eternally been observed that any man who has power is led to abuse it"(Book XI.4), as even virtuous men are inclined to do.

It is in England that Montesquieu sees the model for his ideal government, a government that may not yet be realized. It is in Books XI and XIX that we see how the English constitution provides a solution to the problems associated with human nature; problems which are the result of man's need for security that ends in the infringement on other's liberty unless safeguards are provided by government. As Montesquieu sees it, the problem with earlier governments is that they relied on unreliable attributes of the human character, such as virtue, to bring about a stable government to protect liberty. But in Books XI and XIX Montesquieu never mentions virtue as a necessary component of the English system. In fact, he says that those who founded the English system had no virtue at all (Book III.3). And while he classifies England as a republic and a democracy, it does not have any of those attributes which are unique to republics and democracies, and those attributes are not necessary due to the separation of powers established in its constitution. The human attributes that are relied on are ambition, greed, envy, and jealousy (Book XIX.27), which is what makes the separation of powers work. As the institutions are populated by men with these attributes, the institutions will take on these attributes, which is why the institutions need to be balanced. So as one branch pulls in one direction another pushes against it. The three branches, legislative, executive, and judiciary, balance each other out, resulting in a moderate government, and it is moderate government that provides stability and liberty. This is a lesson Montesquieu learned from his study of history and institutionalized in the separation of powers. Competing interests can come together to form a moderate entity which is better than any interest functioning on its own. Montesquieu did not want to rely on history's progression to bring about liberty in every nation, so he devised a system which could be applied to all nations to bring about liberty. Through the system he has devised, "he narrows the scope and lessens the influence of the deliberate activity of legislators and statesmen" (Pangle 1973, 190).

Section I C.2: Judicial Power

Montesquieu remarks that "the masterwork of legislation is to know where to properly place the power of judging" (Book XI.11). However, this statement about the judiciary is not the norm in Montesquieu's treatment of the judiciary; in fact, he makes his commitment to the judiciary less clear than some readers may like. He does not make his vision of the judiciary explicit, and even glosses over it at times. Book XI deals explicitly with the power of judging in England, but places the general power of judging in the hands of the jury, and offers three exceptions to when the power of judging should not be in the hands of a jury. While he says that the power of judging becomes "invisible and null" when in the hands of the jury, he says nothing of the judiciary being null, and he leaves the question open as to whether the judiciary should be invisible.[20] Montesquieu gives a hint to the "visibility" of the judiciary in Book XIX.27 when he refers to the two visible powers. This reference is directed at the English constitution and the discussion in Book XI. "I have spoken in Book 11 of a free people, and I have given the principles of their constitution . . . in this state there would be two visible powers, the legislative power and the executive power" (Book XIX.27). But when one goes back to Book XI to gain some insight into his vision of the judiciary, and the meaning of this passage, one notices that he does not mention "visible powers" per se, but he does make an effort to mask the judiciary. As Book XI progresses the judiciary becomes conspicuously absent, as the three powers discussed in the opening chapters of Book XI, executive, legislative, and judiciary, become the executive and the two houses of the legislature. Making assumptions about why an author does something can be risky, but I think it is somewhat safe to say that he treats the judiciary in *The Spirit of the Laws* in the same way he would like to see the judiciary operate in a government. That is, he wants to show that the judiciary should operate out of the direct sight of the public, and to some degree the other branches of the government. Reform should be subtle and unobtrusive, and the judiciary is the only branch capable of enacting reforms in this manner. This point is made when he discusses the reform efforts of Saint Louis.

> What is this obscure, confused, and ambiguous code where one constantly mixes French jurisprudence with Roman law; in which one *speaks as a legislator and reveals a jurist*; where one finds a whole body of jurisprudence covering all situations, all the points of civil right? (Book XXVIII.38, italics my own)

The lesson of Book XXVIII is that the judges were the ones who brought about the reforms under Saint Louis.

> Thus the laws made by Saint Louis had effects that could never have been expected of a masterpiece of legislation. Sometimes many centuries pass to prepare for changes; events ripen, and then there are revolutions. (Book XXVIII.39)

This point in Book XXVIII was previously made in Book XXVII when Montesquieu discusses the reform of inheritance laws. As inheritance laws were deeply entrenched within the Roman society, a subtle and unobtrusive method of reform was needed in order to change the laws without much backlash from the public.

> The old Roman law had begun to appear harsh. The praetors were no longer affected except by reasonings of fairness, moderation, and propriety.
>
> The same causes which had restrained the law-keeping women from inheriting had little by little overthrown the one which had hampered inheritance through relatives on the woman's side. These laws were very much in conformity with the spirit of a good republic. (Book XXVII)

These two excerpts combined make the point that it is only through the judiciary and the power of judging that drastic reforms can be implemented without causing civil unrest. Furthermore, these changes that happen little by little are also quite reasonable (Book XXVIII.42–44), and it is only the changes brought about by the judiciary that receive the compliment of being reasonable from Montesquieu.

In addition to being moderate and reasonable, Montesquieu makes other comments about the positive attributes of the judiciary. While he discusses Saint Louis, there are a few passages in which Montesquieu openly addresses the role of the judiciary. He makes it clear that the judiciary is the proper institution to rely on as it is more in accord with the mores and traditions of a society, and it is typically less politically biased than any of the other branches.

> When one saw in his tribunals, and in those of the lords, a more natural, more reasonable way of proceeding, a way more in conformity with morality, religion, public tranquility, and the security of persons and goods, it was taken up and the other was abandoned. (Book XXVIII.38)

The earliest remarks about the judiciary occur in Book II, and in this book Montesquieu states the necessity of having an independent judiciary to prevent despotism, and an independent judiciary may prevent despotism in any form of government. In fact, so long as the laws are protected and there is no infringement on the laws by the government, any form of government will do, but the judiciary is the only branch which can safely protect the rule of law.

> It is not enough to have intermediate ranks in a monarchy; there must also be a depository of laws. This depository can only be in the political bodies, which announce the laws when they are made and recall them when they are forgotten. . . . In despotic states, where there are no fundamental laws, neither is there a depository of laws. (Book II.4)

The power of the judiciary is that it ensures the rule of law by providing a check on other government branches. The judiciary is naturally a moderate political branch, and this moderate tendency will permeate the rest of the government, allowing for liberty to flourish.

> The bodies that are the depository of the laws never obey better than when they drag their feet and bring into the prince's business the reflection that one can hardly expect from the absence of enlightenment in the court concerning the laws of the state and the haste of the prince's councils. (Book V.10)

While none of the three powers is insignificant for Montesquieu's system of governance, it is the judiciary which has the most crucial role. It is the protector of the rule of law, and prevents a backslide into despotism.[21]

The judiciary works because it preserves the positive features of the nobility which existed in the English monarchy. The nobility tied the nation to its past and prevented radical change from the top or the bottom. It served as an anchor which resulted in moderate change.

> Intermediate, subordinate, and dependent powers constitute the nature of monarchical government, that is, of the government in which one alone governs by fundamental laws. . . . The most natural intermediate, subordinate power is that of the nobility. In a way, the nobility is of the essence of monarchy, whose fundamental maxim is: *no monarch, no nobility; no nobility, no monarch;* rather, one has a despot. (Book II.4)

This same role is assumed by the judiciary in Book XXVIII when Montesquieu traces the principle of stare decisis back to the Goths. With the information provided under the separation of powers and judiciary sections, the comparison of the nobility to the judiciary makes the point clear, with respect to my thesis, that Montesquieu sought a system in which man had control, in which there was certainty. While there was no institutional constraint to guarantee that the nobility would serve as that anchor, a judiciary constructed in the manner which Montesquieu advises is a more reliable anchor, as it was through scientifically derived principles that Montesquieu created the philosophical basis for its practical application. Furthermore, while the virtue of men cannot be relied on to counteract and preserve liberty in a monarchy, republic, or democracy, a proper system which balances and divides the formal power of the government will combat the tendency of men and their agencies to expand their power and test the bounds of their authority. For Montesquieu there is much that can go wrong in a system that does not have an extensive set of regulations governing the actions of men, history, or nature, which leads him to devise a system which leaves little to chance by not relying on the above three forces. It is not the institution or the system which is the novel innovation in Montesquieu's work; it is placing man above those effects of nature and history, putting man in a position to control his own fortune. However, Montesquieu never goes so far as to say that man has the capacity to control history, or can eliminate the need for history; he leaves that for Hamilton.

In the following sections that deal with the jurisprudential thought of Blackstone and Hamilton I will show how they were informed by Montesquieu's understanding of history and the role of the judiciary as a stop against the capricious development of history. The principles formulated by Montesquieu were adopted by both Blackstone and Hamilton, but they each took his ideas about man's ability to control government further than Montesquieu was willing to, resulting in a political theory which is different from Montesquieu's but rests firmly in his foundation.

SECTION II: BLACKSTONE

Blackstone's work is an effort to bring a higher level of certainty to the common law through the application of scientific reasoning. The introductory sections of the *Commentaries* continually state that the intention of the work is to bring an enlightened science to the unsystematic state of the common law (1.9, and 1, Introduction, Section 1).[22] His aim for the project is to make the common law systematic. By doing so he attempts to apply scientific principles to the ancient system of common law, as well as combining some of the principles from Roman civil law to the common law. Instead of an inductive system, Blackstone implements first principles in order to make the common law a deductive system so that arguments can be "drawn *a priori*, from the spirit of the laws and the natural foundations of justice" (1, Introduction, Section 1), noting that English law could be "a science, which distinguishes the criterions of right and wrong" (1, Introduction, Section 1). Even more to the point Blackstone wants

> to mark out a Plan of the laws of ENGLAND, so comprehensive, as that every Title might be reduced under some one of its general Heads, which the student might afterwards pursue to any Degree of Minuteness; and at the same time so contracted, that the Gentleman might with tolerable Application contemplate and understand the Whole. (*Analysis*, iv)

So in order to understand Blackstone's teaching one must begin with his assessment of the common law and how he seeks to remedy its deficiencies through the application of scientific principles. After the aims of his project have been established, as well as a sound understanding of the role he gives the judiciary, I will move on to an exploration into Blackstone's reliance on Montesquieu as the source of his progressive jurisprudence. By the end of this section it will be clear that Blackstone's image of the judiciary gives support to the claim that he seeks to place man above history in much the same way that Montesquieu had, but to a greater degree. Montesquieu states that the effects of history can be limited, through the proper application of law. But the law must respect history, thus still maintaining a scheme in which history is superior to human design.

Michael Zuckert makes a remarkable observation: "Partly because of him [Blackstone], the Americans could at once think of political society as the rationalist product of a social compact and as an entity shaped and governed by a law built on custom, deriving its authority from its antiquity and 'grown' character" (Zuckert 2002, 240). Blackstone's rationalism was damaging to the common law. Zuckert puts Blackstone close to many other Enlightenment thinkers when he argues that Blackstone considered England's legal heritage to be an embodiment of philosophical principles. Generalizing from first principles was not what the common law did; that is what Enlightenment thinkers did. To think in this manner is not the artificial reasoning Coke was referring to.[23]

Section II A: Interjecting Scientific Principles and Roman Structure into the Common Law

Since Edward Coke was the single largest figure in common law thought at the time Blackstone was writing, it is no surprise that Blackstone takes on Coke as he is seeking to take on the traditional understanding and application of the common law. Early on in Blackstone's *Commentaries* he attacks Coke by saying that his method is "greatly defective," and that the common law he discusses is nothing more than laws "collected and heaped together." In fact, in all of Coke's writings, Blackstone finds that only one of Coke's four *Institutes* can be considered "methodical" (1, Introduction, Section 3). For Coke, the law is bound by ancient customs and the consciousness of the community, waiting to be discovered, not made, by judges. These statements are made alongside Blackstone's praise of Francis Bacon's new plan for the law. The way he treats Bacon and Coke together mirrors the way he wants the common law and scientific reasoning to be treated together. This pattern of shifting between schools of thought continues throughout the work, and emphasizes the point that there needs to be a balance between common law and science in much the same way that Montesquieu sought a balance between Gothic and Roman law.

Coke is not the only opposition Blackstone finds on his road to reforming traditional common law. John Fortescue is a formidable obstacle to overcome in redefining common law. Like Coke, Fortescue saw no single system, but a compilation of laws.

> If . . . under these three distinctions of the Law of Nature, Customs and Statutes, the fountains and originals of all laws, I shall prove the Law of England eminently excel . . . then I shall have evinced it to be good and effectual for the government of that kingdom. (Fortescue 1825, 47)

To which he added:

> The laws of England, as far as they agree with, and are deduced from the Law of Nature, are neither better nor worse in their decisions than the laws of all other states or kingdoms in similar cases. For, as the philosopher says, in the fifth of his *Ethics*, "The Law of Nature is the same, and has the same force all the world over." (Fortescue 1825, 48)

Coke gives support to this understanding of the common law by saying, "The Law is like a deep well, and he that reacheth deepest seest the amiable and admirable secrets of the Law, wherein the Sages of the Law in ancient Times have had the deepest Reach" (Coke 1979, 71). And in this analysis of the two authors we see the inductive process which animates common law reasoning.

The Roman system of law was quite different from the common law, primarily because of its organized and systematic character. The character of the Roman system was based on deductive reasoning, as opposed to the inductive reasoning of the common law. "The Institutes used the Roman law as a set of pure principles in a deductive way, the deduction being built around the law of nature" (Lobban 1987, 316). But it is not just contemporary authors who have reached this conclusion; Samuel Hallifax says:

> It is admirably calculated to furnish the minds of youth with universal and leading notions . . . the student who confines himself to the institutions of his own country, without joining them any acquaintance with those of Imperial Rome, will never arrive at any considerable skill in the grounds and theory of his profession: though he may perhaps attain to a certain mechanical readiness in the forms and practical parts of the law, he will not be able to comprehend that enlarged and general idea of it, by which it is connected with the great system of Universal Jurisprudence. (Hallifax 1775, x–xii)

John Ayliffe also writes:

> The Law is an Art directing us to the Knowledge of Justice, or *Ars Boni et aequi*, that is to say, a collection of Precepts, teaching us, what is just and what is unjust, what is equitable and what savors of Iniquity. For the word *Art* here signifies a system of certain propositions, *viz*, which are known to us by Practice and which lead Men to some profitable End of Life. . . . Persons ought not immediately in the beginning to commit themselves rashly to the Ocean, but to set out in their Searches after this Knowledge from self-evident principles, and from the Elements of the Law. (Ayliffe 1734, 2–3)

The impact the Roman system of legal reasoning and scientific inquiry had on Blackstone becomes obvious when we read in Blackstone that:

> reason with precision, and separate argument from fallacy, by the clear simple rules of pure unsophisticated logic; if he can fix his attention, and steadily pursue truth through any the most intricate deduction, by the use of mathematical demonstrations; if he has enlarged his conceptions . . . by a view of the several branches of genuine, experimental, philosophy; if he has impressed on his mind the sound maxims of the law of nature, the best and most authentic foundation of human laws; if, lastly, he has contemplated those maxims reduced to a practical system in the laws of imperial Rome . . . a student thus qualified may enter upon the study of law. (1, Introduction, Section 1)

Thus, when the contradictions that exist between the Roman and common law system are understood, one begins to understand why Blackstone had to change the nature of the judiciary in the way that he did; since his aim was to adapt the Roman system to the English common law system, the compromise forced him to change the nature of judging from something which found the law to something which made the law.

Blackstone struggles with the need to balance two principles that do not necessarily complement each other or lend themselves to being conjoined with one another: the historic foundations of law, as displayed in common law, and reason, as displayed in the Roman system. His concern for history implies that he understands how history can shape men and institutions, much in the same way that Montesquieu understood the effect. Blackstone spends a fair amount of time discussing the history of British common law, but his ambition of making the common law systematic forces him to limit the role of history, as it is the impact of history through custom and tradition that establishes the character of common law.[24] Blackstone departs from other common law scholars when he tries to explain the development of the law through reason, in order to understand the principles behind the law, so that a rational explanation can be achieved. Once this rational explanation has been achieved, and first principles extracted, the law can be applied universally, according to Blackstone, in order to promote liberty and justice through the law.

Blackstone does not expend much effort giving his own definition of natural law; instead he relies on other writers, such as Pufendorf, for his definition. When he states his definition of natural law he says:

> As God, when he created matter, endued it with a principle of mobility, established certain rules for the perpetual direction of that motion; so, when he created man, and endued him with freewill to conduct himself in all parts of life, he laid down certain immutable laws of nature, whereby that freewill is to some degree regulation and restrained, and gave him also the faculty of reason to discover the purport of those laws. (1, Introduction, Section 2)

Blackstone gives the impression that the natural law exists, but that it requires reason to discover it. This is perhaps why he abandons the common law of Fortescue and Coke, as they do not rely on reason to understand the law. Nested within this definition is the implication that natural law cannot enforce itself, and requires human law that is in accord with reason, and thus natural law, to enforce it. Thus, natural law is created by God, but requires man to make it real in the sense that a law that is not enforced or known does not serve the purpose of law, which is to restrain and direct behavior which upsets civil society. In fact, he spends much effort in the first sections of the first volume expressing the opinion that natural law only has force once it is converted into human law. The scope of natural law is severely restricted once it becomes human law, as human law only concerns itself with social factors.

Human laws can have no concern with any but social and relative duties, being intended only to regulate the conduct of man, considered under various relations, as a member of civil society. All crimes ought therefore to be estimated merely according to the mischiefs which they produce in civil society: and of consequence private vices, or the breach of mere absolute duties which man is bound to perform considered only as an individual, are not, cannot be, the object of any municipal law (4, Section 1).

By defining and applying natural law in this way, he gives more authority and flexibility to human law, which then places the ultimate law-making authority in the hands of man. Blackstone makes this clear when he says, "there is and must be in all of them a supreme, irresistible, absolute, uncontrolled authority, in which the *jura summi imperii*, or the rights of the sovereignty, reside" (1, Introduction, Section 2). Since the parliament is the most visible law-making authority in England, it is only natural to think that Blackstone was referring to parliament. Supporting this idea, Blackstone mentions that "If the parliament will positively enact a thing to be done which is unreasonable, I know of no power that can control it" (1, Introduction, Section 3). But the interesting term in this excerpt is "can," not should or ought. Just as Montesquieu is writing to the statesman, Blackstone is writing for the judiciary, as his lectures to classes in the legal academy are what form the foundation of the *Commentaries*. This gives one an idea that perhaps he is trying to instruct the judiciary on how to reform law without coming into direct confrontation with the parliament. He has already been able to eliminate natural law as an impediment to man-made law; now he must overcome the parliament's obstruction to the judiciary's power in order to establish the judiciary as the supreme law-making authority.

As a result of Blackstone's ambition to bring about a systematic understanding of the law, first principles, and a universal application, he creates a legal positivism that is more closely linked with Hobbes than the common law tradition of Coke, Fortescue, or Aristotle. According to Blackstone, the common law "is positive law, fixed and established by custom, which custom is evidenced by judicial decisions" (1, Introduction, Section 3). In the introduction to the *Commentaries* Blackstone makes the point of giving judges control over the common law. When he raises the question of who has authority over the common law he says:

> The answer is, by the judges of the several courts of justice. They are the depositary of the laws; the living oracles, who must decide in all cases of doubt, and who are bound by an oath to decide according to the law of the land. . . . And indeed these judicial decisions are the principle and most authoritative evidence, that can be given, of the existence of such a custom as shall form a part of the common law. (1, Introduction, Section 3)

This says that judges decide what the common law is, and without judges the common law would not be known. His thoughts on the common law remain conservative, but in his discussion of the role of precedent his positivist inclinations become more evident when he writes:

> For it is an established rule to abide by former precedents, where the same points come again in litigation; as well to keep the scale of justice even and steady, and not liable to waver with every new judge's opinion; as also because the law in that case being solemnly declared and determined, what before was uncertain, and perhaps indifferent, is now become a permanent rule, which it is not in the breast of any subsequent judge to alter or vary from . . . he being sworn to determine . . . according to the known laws and customs of the land. (1, Introduction, Section 3)

In unpacking this section from Blackstone, Paul Carrese points out that "The reasons given for adhering to precedent . . . stem less from a revealed or natural law separately conceived than from principles of proper procedure" (Carrese 2003, 141). This is an important point to understand; since Blackstone is seeking a system which is universally applicable he needs institutions and procedures that carry out the principles he devises from his study of history, since without those institutions and procedures the application would rely solely on custom and tradition, and if those customs and traditions are lacking, then the principles become inapplicable. But with the proper institutions and procedures which minimize the effect of customs and traditions, thus minimizing the effect of history, Blackstone can apply his first principles in any environment regardless of history. Therefore, in order to make his system applicable he needs a system of implementation as well, and in this case the role is partially served by precedent. This is drawing closer to the idea that Blackstone thinks that he can devise a system which can control history through the proper application of scientifically derived first principles. Note the difference in the role of precedent in Blackstone and traditional common law. Blackstone sees precedent as a tool of overcoming tradition and custom and a way of instituting reform, whereas traditional common law used precedent as a restraint on judges.

The way Blackstone applies the terms reason and scientifically derived principles, the terms are made nearly synonymous. So when he says that law must be in accord with reason in order to be law, he is making the point that reason is the knowledge, or those first principles, which is the result of scientific inquiry. To make the point that law must be in accord with reason Blackstone writes that the rule of precedent may be violated if the precedent is a bad one.

> Yet this rule admits of exception, where the former determination is most evidently contrary to reason; much more if it be contrary to divine law. But even in such cases the subsequent judges do not pretend to make a new law, but to vindicate the old one from misrepresentation. For if it be found . . . manifestly absurd or unjust it is declared, not that such a sentence is bad law, but that it is not law . . . the law is the perfection of reason, that it always intends to conform thereto, and that what is not reason is not law. (1, Introduction, Section 3)

This, however, seems at odds with the previous assertion that Blackstone is a legal positivist. Here he seems to say that law handed down by the sovereign may be declared not law at all, something Hobbes would surely scoff at. But the completeness of Blackstone's thought should not be so hastily determined; as we look further into the text, it is shown that Blackstone reconciles his "what is not reason is not law" maxim with the sovereign's unhindered ability to declare law.

> The doctrine of the law then is this: that precedents and rules must be followed, unless flatly absurd or unjust: for though their reason be not obvious at first view, yet we owe such a deference to former times as not to suppose they acted wholly without consideration. (1, Introduction, Section 3)

Blackstone still leaves an out, so to speak, against the absolute power of the sovereign to declare law. However, when Blackstone is pressed by the reader, the reader sees that it is not the power of the sovereign that he wishes to limit, but the power of the parliament, and then he shifts power to the judiciary which would then declare law, but a declaratory power which is checked by the parliament and other institutional constraints.[25] By providing a sovereign in the form of the judiciary who is free to declare law, Blackstone becomes more of a positivist than either the Roman or common law traditions would allow since the judiciary he created would need neither to deduce nor discover law, but only impose the law.

Blackstone slowly converts common law into positive law. Once he has done so, he has given judges the authority to make positive law: "Upon the whole however, we may take it as a general rule, 'that the decisions of courts of justice are the evidence of what is common law': in the same manner as, in the civil law, what the emperor had once determined was to serve for a guide for the future" (1, Introduction, Section 3). Blackstone's change is subtle, but we only need to revisit the natural law understanding of common law found in Coke and Fortescue to realize that equating the court's power to an emperor is an inaccurate estimation of the authority of a common law court. The court does not determine what the guide for the future is; the court is guided by reason and past decisions. This is a difference that may be linked to the influence of Montesquieu. Blackstone now gives judges control over the common law, whereas before it was history which controlled common law. So by giving judges control over common law, he gives man control over the influence that history can have on political development.

Once Blackstone provides the theoretical grounding judges need to make positive law, he gives them the tools to do so. Blackstone gives judges greater latitude in deciding the law by giving them the power to make decisions in equity, and the guidelines for equity power that he provides allows judges to expand their authority as law makers, but Blackstone is still a moderate reformer not yet prepared to turn the reins over to the judiciary completely. He would still like to see the actions of the judiciary checked by their own practices and by the actions of the legislature. Blackstone makes this clear when he says, "there should be somewhere be a power vested of excepting those circumstances which the legislator himself would have excepted," but equity should not be handed over unchecked: "And law, without equity, though hard and disagreeable, is much more desirable for the public good, than equity without law" (1, Introduction, Section 2). But the decision on whether to give equity authority over law begins to get confused: "These are the several grounds of the laws of England: over and above which, equity is frequently called in to assist, to moderate, and to explain" (1, Introduction, Section 3). He goes on to say that the authority to make decisions in equity should not, and does not, reside solely in the courts of equity, but that common law judges make decisions "according to the spirit of the rule" (4, Section 1, paraphrasing Montesquieu Book VI.2 and Book III.27). Blackstone seems to get even bolder in his claims concerning equity as he says, "Equity then, in its true and genuine meaning, is the soul and spirit of all law: positive law is construed, and rational law is made, by it. In this, equity is synonymous to justice, in that equity is the true sense and sound interpretation of the rule (3, Section 2). With the information given up to this point the following conclusion can be drawn. Natural law is not relevant without first becoming human law. Human law and positive law are both to be understood as meaning the same thing, as human law is the foundation for civil society and therefore needs to be posited by the sovereign; otherwise it remains natural law. The judiciary can make positive law, and through its use of equity, which is "synonymous with justice," the judiciary is given authority over parliament. Thus, law and justice rest in the hands of judges, no longer determined by history or natural law. History, in the form of precedent, custom, and tradition, is no longer needed as a guide for judges once a formal system of rules and first principles has been established, and positive laws, which are in accord with reason, have been implemented.

Section II B: Similarities between Blackstone and Montesquieu

Blackstone lays out his project much in the same way Montesquieu does and seems to adopt Montesquieu's definition of the spirit of the laws.

> These originals should be traced to their fountains . . . to the customs of the Britons and Germans . . . to the codes of the northern nations . . . to the rules of the Roman law . . . but, above all, to that inexhaustible reservoir of legal antiquities and learning, the feudal law . . . the law of nations in the Western orb. The primary rules and fundamental principles should be weighed and compared with the precepts of the law of nature, and the practice of other countries, should be explained by reasons, illustrated by examples, and confirmed by undoubted authorities; their history should be deduced, their changes and revolutions observed, and it should be shown how far they are connected with, or have at any

time been affected by, the civil transactions of the kingdom. (1, Introduction, Section 1; see Montesquieu Book I.3)

This indicates that the central focus of both authors is on laws and how a uniform system of law derived from first principles can be adapted to different environments whose history must be recognized and respected so as not to incite resistance to the new laws whose aim is the promotion of liberty and stability.[26]

The most notable similarity between Blackstone and Montesquieu, as far as this study is concerned, has to do with the judiciary, as it is the judiciary which will be responsible for implementing the new laws in a moderate way. For both men the judiciary is the depository of the laws, and serves as a moderating influence within government, balancing all of the other forces. In Books II and VI, Montesquieu offers passages that make judges the depositories of the laws much in the same way Blackstone does in the third section of his first book. But the most striking instance comes when Blackstone writes:

> For the freedom of our constitution will not permit, that in criminal cases a power should be lodged in any judge, to construe the law otherwise than according to the letter. This caution, while it admirably protects the public liberty, can never bear hard upon individuals. A man cannot suffer more punishment than the law assigns, but he may suffer less. (1, Introduction, Section 3)

This excerpt is strikingly similar to passages found in Books II, V, VI, and XXVIII. This sentiment is also echoed in Books II.4, V.11, and XXVIII.45. More specifically, Montesquieu, in discussing despotism, says:

> Therefore, all occasions for disputes and proceedings are taken away there [in despotic governments]. This is, in part, what makes pleaders so mistreated; the injustice of their request appears badly, being neither hidden, mitigated, nor protected by an affinity of laws. (Book VI.1)

In addition to their complimentary outlook on judicial power, the role of the judiciary is also similar in the sense that it serves as a balancing force for both authors. Where Blackstone says the judiciary is to serve as a third branch that supports "the rights of both the crown and the people, by forming a barrier to withstand the encroachments of both," and without that third branch, stability would be threatened since the swings in power would be too great to bear. Montesquieu reiterates this point throughout *The Spirit of the Laws*, but it is in Books III.7 and III.9 that the most obvious connection between Blackstone and Montesquieu exists on this point. And in addition to these examples, Blackstone gives direct citations of Montesquieu in his last book, which discusses judicial power as a protector of the people.

The similarities between Blackstone and Montesquieu extend beyond the treatment of the judiciary in general to include how the judiciary will function with a system of separated powers. Blackstone discusses the separation of powers principle when he discusses the benefits of mixed regimes and in his praise of the British constitution. Blackstone says, in reference to the British constitution and its system of separated powers, that each branch "is actuated by different springs, and attentive to different interests . . . in no other shape could we be so certain of finding the three great qualities of government so well and so happily united . . . virtue, wisdom, or power"(1, Introduction, Section 2). This statement mirrors the sentiment of Montesquieu in Book XI.6 and 12–19, and we even see a glimpse of this idea earlier in Book III.3.[27] Much like Montesquieu, Blackstone asserts that "the true excellence of the English government is that all the parts of it form a mutual check upon each other . . . every branch of our civil polity supports and is supported, regulates and is regulated, by the rest" (1, Section 2). Blackstone makes his adaptation of Montesquieu even more explicit when he writes:

> Like three powers in mechanics, they jointly impel the machine of government in a direction different from what either, acting by themselves, would have done; but at the same time in a direction partaking of each, and formed out of all; a direction which constitutes the true line of liberty and happiness of the community. (1, Section 2)

Furthermore, the judiciary is treated by both authors somewhat deceptively as neither author includes it as a vital part throughout their discussion of the separation of powers, sometimes including it, sometimes substituting it with another branch, and other times dropping it altogether. But in one of the places that Blackstone does make the judiciary's role within the separation of powers explicit he calls the judiciary "the grand depository of the fundamental laws of the kingdom," and calls for the "administration of common justice to be in some degree separated from the legislative and also from the executive power" (1, Section 3). The issue of Montesquieu's treatment of the judiciary has been discussed in an earlier section, and the central importance of the judiciary to Blackstone has been discussed above as well. What is unclear is why Blackstone would treat the judiciary in a fashion similar to Montesquieu, unless he too wished for the judiciary to act in a less visible manner than the legislative and executive branches. Unfortunately, there is no sufficient answer to why Blackstone does this; all that is available are examples where he does. (Compare 1.2 in the *Commentaries* to Book XI in *The Spirit of the Laws*.)

Throughout his discussion of the separation of powers Blackstone weaves the judiciary in and out of the discussion in much the same way that Montesquieu does in his discussion of the English constitution, making it difficult to track their discussion of the judiciary. But, in addition to the examples already provided, similarities in how these authors envision the role of the judiciary can be found in each of their discussions of successful reformers. Just as Montesquieu attributes the success of Saint Louis to his subtleness in conjoining laws and the use of the judiciary to enact moderate reforms gradually, Blackstone uses Edward I and Chief Justice Mansfield. For Blackstone, Mansfield continued the reform efforts of Edward I, who laid the groundwork for substantive due process and the use of equity as a source for judicial power. It was the power of equity in the court that allowed Edward I to enact reforms during the reign of Henry VIII (4, Sections 32–33). It was the equity power of the courts that allowed for the correction and gradual adoption of reforms brought by Charles II. The legacy of Edward I was to be found by Blackstone in Mansfield, whose

> liberality of sentiment which now has taken possession of our courts of common law, and induced them to adopt the same principles of redress as have prevailed in our courts of equity . . . by extending the remedial influence of the equitable writ of trespass on the case, according to its primitive institution by King Edward the First, to almost every instance of injustice not remedied by any other process. (4, Section 33)

Through his analysis then of the tradition established initially by the Saxon Alfred and restored by Edward I and perpetuated by Mansfield, Blackstone is making the same argument that Montesquieu made in his analysis of Saint Louis. Moderate reforms are best adapted through the judiciary as they tend to work slowly and respect the traditions and consciousness of the community. In both Montesquieu and Blackstone it is important to recognize that the reforms brought about protected the liberty of the people, but the reforms were not demanded by the people or even desired by the people; they were the acts of great men. Thus, the aim of Montesquieu and Blackstone is to somehow institutionalize the process used by Louis, Edward I, and Mansfield.

Blackstone's project is an attempt at bringing a systematic mode of law to England by adapting Roman law to the English common law. In so doing, he made changes to the judiciary and the classic understanding of common law. His reforms to the understanding of traditional common law transformed judges from interpreters of the law into makers of the law. Traditionally judges tried to find the spirit, or the letter, of the law through an inductive process which included long, laborious study. Through stare decisis the dialectic occurred in which extremes were avoided and a natural balancing effect occurred. This process was too unreliable and unsystematic for Blackstone. While he supported the moderating tendency of stare decisis, he needed something which could be institutionalized so as to be consistent with his aim of establishing an ordered system of law. What resulted, whether intentional or not, was a transformation of the common law into positive law, with judges as the makers of the law. Due to the training of the men who filled the judiciary, and the institutional limitations of the judiciary enforced by the other branches of government, judges would take the place of the dialectic as the moderating force of the law, replacing the customs and tradition that went into the dialectic associated with stare decisis and common law. In Blackstone we see more reliance on institutions and reason and a further abandonment of history than we did in Montesquieu; Hamilton will continue this progression by further pushing the principles of Montesquieu until he arrives at a system which is nearly devoid of reliance on history.

SECTION III: HAMILTON

One cannot deny the influence Montesquieu and Blackstone had on the thinking of the American founders. These two men were cited more than any other Enlightenment thinker. Moreover, if we are looking for an indication of America's departure from the English common law the reader should recognize that Blackstone is referenced six more times than Coke by the founding fathers. However, such a superficial analysis will never do to convince the discerning reader, and even if it could it leaves too many questions unexplored to be interesting. Furthermore, the founding fathers were more than scribes; they were political philosophers in their own right.

Whereas Montesquieu and Blackstone used history as a tool to transmit their teachings and as the basis for their philosophy, Hamilton sought a clean break with the systems of the past in an effort to create a system founded on a new political science. Montesquieu sought to replicate history in his system of separated powers, and he attempted to use the judiciary as a facilitator of moderation much in the same way history had functioned to balance the extremes. He learned from history how things naturally progressed, and institutionalized those lessons into a system of governance so as to create a government that would achieve liberty without having to rely on fate or fall victim to the unpredictability of history. Blackstone saw history in much the same way as Montesquieu had but limited the role of history more than Montesquieu had. Even after Montesquieu establishes his new system, he does not deny that history and other factors can still affect the character of a people, which is why he says it is the job of a good ruler, or a good system, to adapt to these variables. Blackstone, however, seems to say that when the system he has created is implemented, there is no room for outside forces to become involved, as all variables are controlled for in a proper system. When we arrive at Hamilton we find a thinker who considers all previous attempts at governance to be failures. Hamilton thinks that the system created by the U.S. Constitution is far superior to any that has existed before and it is because of the advances of the science of politics that has allowed the Founders to isolate and correct the deficiencies of past republics. Hamilton sees no reason to adapt the lessons of history; instead he seeks a clean break. Hamilton falls in line with the two earlier thinkers in relying on the proper institutional design to perpetuate a strong system of government. In his writings Hamilton does not rely on the virtue of the rulers or the people; instead he seeks to replace the need for virtue with institutional design. The institutional design proposed by Hamilton is heavily influenced by Montesquieu's separation of powers design, and he uses the judiciary in much the same way as both Montesquieu and Blackstone. The judiciary serves as the moderating force for all three men. While it is accepted knowledge that Montesquieu and Blackstone had some influence on the thought of all the Founders, not just Hamilton, it is Hamilton who follows most closely the teachings of Montesquieu and Blackstone.

Section III A: Abandonment of Historical Lessons in the Creation of a New Political Science

While Montesquieu and Blackstone both use historical examples to make their point about the need for various reforms, and to transmit their philosophical teachings, Hamilton—and Publius as a whole—uses historical examples only to show that the past attempts at governance have been wrong, which is why a new political science is called for. For Hamilton the only lesson to be taken from history is that we should not duplicate what has been done before, and instead build on a new foundation in order to make a new system of politics that is better than any system previously known. According to Judith Shklar's reading of *The Federalist Papers*, "The new political science could [according to Publius], properly applied, build a self-correcting system of government that would not suffer any of the infirmities that had afflicted the older systems" (Shklar 1977, 1290). Hamilton is almost irreverent when he talks about the attempts at governance that have come before:

> It is impossible to read the history of the petty republics of Greece and Italy, without feeling the sensations of horror and disgust at the distractions with which they were continually agitated, and at the rapid succession of revolutions, by which they were kept perpetually vibrating between the extremes of tyranny and anarchy. If they exhibit occasional calms, these only serve as short-lived

> contrasts to the furious storms that are to succeed. . . . The science of politics, however, like most other sciences, has received great improvement. The efficacy of various principles is now well understood, which were either not known at all, or imperfectly known to the ancients. (*Federalist* 9, 37–38)[28]

When Hamilton discusses earlier theorists who advocated republics, he gives examples of the republics these men advocated in order to show the deficiencies in earlier theories as well as earlier attempts at republican government.

> The genius of republics, say they, is pacific; the spirit of commerce has a tendency to soften the manners of men. . . . Sparta, Athens, Rome, and Carthage, were all republics; two of them, Athens and Carthage, of the commercial kind. Yet were they as often engaged in wars, offensive and defensive, as the neighboring monarchies of the same time. Sparta was little better than a well regulated camp; and Rome was never sated of carnage and conquest.
>
> Carthage, though a commercial republic, was the aggressor in the very war that ended in her destruction. . . . Venice, in latter times, figured more than once in wars of ambition. . . . The provinces of Holland, till they were overwhelmed in debts and taxes, too a leading and conspicuous part in the wars of Europe. (*Federalist* 6, 23–24)

Even James Madison was compelled to get into the action of breaking with the past.

> The novelty of the undertaking immediately strikes us. It has been shown in the course of these papers that the existing confederation is founded on principles which are fallacious; that we must consequently change this first foundation, and with it the superstructure resting upon it. It has been shown that the other confederacies which could be consulted as precedents have been vitiated by the same erroneous principles, and can therefore furnish no other light than beacons, which give warning of the course to be shunned. (*Federalist* 37, 180–81)

According to Hamilton and his coauthors, the primary failure of previous republics was their inability to characterize human nature correctly, which then prohibited them from creating the institutions that would use human nature in such a way that would lead to a successful governing system. Hamilton argues that the superiority of the Constitution to the ancient republics is based upon the "great improvements," in modern times, achieved in the "science of politics" (*Federalist* 9).

Section III A.1: The Failure of the Ancients to Understand Human Nature and the Founders' Ability to Create a Government That Could Control the Negative Effects of Human Nature

For Hamilton, human nature is dominated by passion, which is to imply that vice is more dominant than virtue, and passion is more dominant than reason, and though there is no willingness to link virtue to reason, he clearly links vice to passion. According to Hamilton, men are "ambitious, vindictive, and rapacious" (*Federalist* 6, 21). In *Federalist* 55, Madison, who tends to be more guarded and optimistic than Hamilton, recognizes that men are more often guided by passion, which makes necessary a government structure that can promote reasonable solutions in the face of competing passions.

> Had every Athenian citizen been a Socrates, every Athenian assembly would still have been a mob. . . . As there is a degree of depravity in mankind, which requires a certain degree of circumspection and distrust, so there are other qualities in human nature, which justify a certain portion of esteem and confidence. Republican government presupposes the existence of these qualities in a higher degree than any other form. (*Federalist* 55, 288 and 291)

But even before Madison makes this comment, Hamilton answers the question of why government is necessary by saying, "Because the passions of men will not conform to the dictates of reason and justice, without constraint." (*Federalist* 15, 73).

Hamilton makes his most explicit comments on human nature and its effects at the Philadelphia Convention. As Robert Yates reports, Hamilton says:

> Take mankind in general, they are vicious. . . . Take mankind as they are, and what are they governed by? Their passions. There may be in every government a few choice spirits, who may act from more worthy motives. One great error is that we suppose mankind more honest than they are. Our prevailing passions are ambition and interest; it will ever be the duty of a wise government to avail itself of these passions, in order to make them subservient to the public good. (Farrand 1911, vol. 1, 388–89)

In a letter to James A. Bayard written after the Constitution had been ratified, Hamilton remarks again on man's nature.

> Nothing is more fallacious than to expect to produce any valuable or permanent result in political projects by relying merely on the reason of men. Men are rather reasoning than reasonable animals, for the most part governed by the impulse of passion . . . the strongest and most active passion of the human heart, vanity. (Lodge 1885–1886, 597)

And according to Hamilton and his most recognized coauthor, Madison, it was precisely this understanding of human nature that escaped the ancients, and the misunderstanding of the ancients left no option but for their governments to be destroyed by the manifestations of the vices in human nature, most notably through factions, since they did not provide any correction for human nature (*Federalist* 9, 10, 15, 51, and 72). While Madison is most commonly cited as recognizing the debilitating effects of factions, it was Hamilton who wrote, "A spirit of faction, which is apt to mingle its poison in the deliberations of all bodies of men, will often hurry the persons, of whom they are composed, into improprieties and excesses, for which they would blush in a private capacity" (*Federalist* 15, 73).

While human nature could be destructive, Hamilton saw an opportunity to create a system based on a proper understanding of human nature that would lead to a stable government. In a critique of the ancients, and in promoting his vision of how the Constitution would work, Hamilton says that

> the difference between the true politician and the political-empyric is this: the later will . . . attempt to travel out of human nature and introduce institutions and projects for which man is not fitted. . . . The true politician . . . takes human nature as he finds it, a compound of good and ill qualities. . . . With this view of human nature he will not attempt to warp or distort it from it natural direction. (Morris 1957, 313–14)[29]

Men's passions can be made useful by pitting passion against passion in an institutionalized and controlled format. When discussing the reeligibility of the president, Hamilton shows how different passions can counteract each other in order to reach good policy.

> Even the love of fame, the ruling passion of the noblest minds, which would prompt a man to plan and undertake extensive and arduous enterprises for the public benefit, requiring considerable time to mature and perfect them, if he could flatter himself with the prospect of being allowed to finish what he had begun, would, on the contrary, deter him from undertaking, when he foresaw that he must quit the scene before he could accomplish his work. . . . Add to this, that the same man might be vain or ambitious as well as avaricious. And if he could expect to prolong his honors by his good conduct, he might hesitate to sacrifice his appetite for them [passions], to his appetite for gain. (*Federalist* 72, 375–76)

Throughout Hamilton's discussion of how the separation of powers will work and how each branch will be tied to the promotion of the public good, he relies on man's pride, ambition, vanity, and other vices that usually animate the actions of men who take office. And it is through controlling these vices that the public good will be elevated above individual self-interest. At the convention Hamilton makes this point when he says:

> In every community where industry in encouraged, there will be a division of it into a few and the many. Hence, separate interests will arise. . . . Give all power to the many, they will oppress the few. Give all power to the few, they will oppress the many. Both, therefore, ought to have the power, that each may defend itself against the other. (Farrand 1911, vol. 1, 371)

For Hamilton, the real challenge in forming a stable government that inhibits tyranny is finding the proper balance. In each branch of government and within each interest in society there is a vice, and these vices can be balanced by the vices of the competing branches and interests.

The balancing in government occurs then, because the powers of the executive, legislative, and judging are separated just as Montesquieu advised and Blackstone reaffirmed. An example of how this system works, and why it works, can be found in Hamilton's comments in *Federalist* 66:

> An absolute or qualified negative in the executive, upon the acts of the legislative body, is admitted by the ablest adepts in political science, to be an indispensable barrier against the encroachments of the latter upon the former. And it may . . . be contended, that the powers relating to impeachments are . . . an essential check in the hands of that body, upon the encroachments of the executive. (*Federalist* 66, 342–43)

Of course, the bulk of the *Federalist Papers* describe how the new system will work, so making reference to all relevant citations with regard to separation of powers would be a bit tedious, but a few references to offer support to my claims makes sense. There are institutional mechanisms within the legislature which allow it to check the actions of the executive: "The legislature, with a discretionary power over the salary and emoluments of the chief magistrate, could render him obsequious to their will, as they might think proper to make him" (*Federalist* 73, 379). And the power of the purse also checks the judiciary (*Federalist* 79). Similarly, the courts (*Federalist* 78) and the executive (*Federalist* 66) have institutionalized mechanisms to check the legislature, and each other (*Federalist* 81). The men in each branch are expected to have passions that can overwhelm reason, and the institutions are formulated in such a way that the passions within each branch will counteract the passions of the other branches, much in the same way *Federalist* 51 says that ambition is made to counteract ambition.

Section III B: A Judiciary Based on the Lessons of a New Political Science

There are five principles presented by Hamilton which were either unknown or incorrectly known by the ancients. For Publius the success of American constitutionalism would hinge on the separation of powers, a bicameral legislature, elected representatives, and federalism properly applied. Hamilton agrees with his coauthors that these four principles are crucial, but he adds a fifth, the courts, which Hamilton places above the other four as being central to the success of the project.

> The science of politics, however, like most other sciences, has received great improvement. The efficacy of various principles is now well understood, which were either not known at all, or imperfectly known to the ancients. The regular distribution of power into distinct departments; the introduction of legislative balances and checks; the institution of the courts composed of the judges, holding their offices during good behavior; the representation of the people in the legislature, by deputies of their own election; these are either wholly new discoveries, or have made their principal progress towards perfection in modern times. They are means, and powerful means, by which the excellence of republican government may be retained, and it imperfections lessened or avoided. (*Federalist* 9, 38)

Not only did ancient republics not understand these principles, the Articles of Confederation, which the Constitution was intended to replace, did not apply these new principles. Hamilton was worried about how the rule of law would survive in the earlier American confederation since it lacked a strong judiciary, and a strong judiciary was important since the administration of the laws is the "cement of society" (*Federalist* 17, 82). He goes so far to say that the want of a judiciary power in the earlier American confederacy is its chief defect.

> A circumstance which crowns the defects of the confederation remains yet to be mentioned . . . the want of a judiciary power. Laws are a dead letter, without courts to expound and define their true meaning and operation. . . . Their true import, as far as respects individuals, must, like all other laws, be ascertained by judicial determinations. To produce uniformity in these determinations, they ought to be submitted, in the last resort, to one SUPREME TRIBUNAL. . . . To avoid the confusion which would unavoidably result from the contradictory decisions of a number of independent judicatories, all nations have found it necessary to establish one tribunal paramount to the rest, possessing a general superintendence, and authorized to settle and declare in the last resort an uniform rule of civil justice. (*Federalist* 22, 110)

This passage reflects not only the central importance the judiciary serves in Hamilton's thought, but also how far his thought has departed from traditional common law thinking to approximate the liberal thought of Blackstone. First, uniformity is inimical to the common law tradition; a central characteristic of common law was its adaptability to local interests, something uniformity cannot accomplish unless all local interests are uniform. Second, "one tribunal paramount to the rest" is not a common law system. Common law courts were by definition local courts that made decisions at the community level; they were intended to handle matters of justice which central powers could not handle adequately. Last, in the common law tradition, courts do not "declare" law or a "uniform rule of civil justice." The idea that courts can declare law is direct evidence of the influence of Blackstone's theory of a judiciary which is the sovereign lawmaker.

Throughout his writings as Publius, Hamilton places the judiciary at the heart of government. It is the judiciary which serves as the moderating force between the other two branches and between minority and majority factions.

> It is far more rational to suppose that the courts were designed to be an intermediate body between the people and the legislature, in order, among other things, to keep the latter within the limits assigned to their authority . . . the judicial magistracy is certainly one of the most valuable modern improvements in the practice of government.[30] In a monarchy, it is an excellent barrier to the despotism of a prince: in a republic it is a no less excellent barrier to the encroachments and oppressions of the representative body. And it is the best expedient which can be devised in any government, to secure a steady, upright, and impartial administration of the laws. (*Federalist* 78, 402)[31]

The judiciary is treated as, in Blackstone's terms, the depository of the law. But even more than a depository, the judiciary takes an active role in holding the system stable and maintaining national supremacy. The authority granted to the federal judiciary becomes undeniable when one reads closely. When Hamilton is writing about the need for the national government to have superiority over the state governments, it is through the judiciary that this can most successfully be accomplished.

> It must stand in need of no intermediate legislations; but must itself be empowered to employ the arm of the magistrate to execute its own resolutions. *The majesty of the national authority must be manifested through the medium of the courts of justice*. The government of the union . . . must be able to address itself immediately to the hopes and fears of individuals; and to attract to its support, those passions, which have the strongest influence upon the heart. It must, in short, possess all the means, and have a right to resort to all the methods, of

> executing the powers with which it is entrusted, that are possessed and exercised by the governments of the particular states. (*Federalist* 16, 78, italics my own)[32]

As was seen in *Federalist* 22, it is through the federal courts that uniformity in the laws will be maintained, and this uniformity will help tie the people to the national government. The need for uniformity in interpretation of the laws is repeated in *Federalist* 80, when he compares thirteen states with their own power of interpretation to a hydra. In *Federalist* 80, he makes it a point to state that the power of the judiciary must be at least equal to that of the legislature. But he seems to place the judiciary above the legislature when he gives the court power to review legislative actions, but then quickly denies that judicial review would give the judiciary supremacy over the legislature. "Nor does this conclusion by any means suppose a superiority to the intention of the judicial to the legislative power" (*Federalist* 78, 404).

Hamilton's treatment of the judiciary in *Federalist* 78 is not quite convincing. I say this because he continually states that the judiciary will not be able to exert its will over the legislature or the Constitution, but the argument progresses in such a way that one is almost forced to draw the conclusion that the judiciary does in fact have control over both the legislature and the Constitution. First, the Constitution is the supreme law. "No legislative act therefore contrary to the constitution can be valid. . . . A constitution is in fact, and must be, regarded by the judges as a fundamental law" (*Federalist* 78, 403 and 404). Second, the judiciary makes all decisions when there is a constitutional question. "It therefore belongs to them [the courts] to ascertain its [constitution's] meaning as well as the meaning of any particular act proceeding from the legislative body" (*Federalist* 78, 404).

Furthermore, the judiciary has the power to determine which of two contradictory laws is valid. Finally, judges are free to make decisions according to their will. Hamilton warns that "The courts must declare the sense of the law; and if they should be disposed to exercise WILL instead of JUDGMENT, the consequence would equally be the substitution of their pleasure to that of the legislative body" (*Federalist* 78, 405). One might expect Hamilton to follow this up with some restriction to prevent judges from making judgments according to their will, or some condemnation of judges who do exercise their will, but he provides neither. What Hamilton leaves us with is this: The Constitution is supreme law, making statute law subordinate to the Constitution, which makes the legislature subordinate to the Constitution since the legislature's authority arises from their ability to make statutes. The Court decides the meaning of the Constitution, which means that the meaning of the Constitution is defined by the court as there is no reference to higher law which would hold the meaning of the Constitution stable. Since the judiciary defines the Constitution, judges have authority over the Constitution, thus giving them power over the legislature and statutes, as the power to define seems to be the power to control when it comes to constitutionalism. Furthermore, there is no restriction placed on the judiciary which would prevent it from enforcing its will upon the Constitution, nor is there punishment for doing so. In fact, "The rules of legal interpretation, are rules of *common sense*, adopted by the courts in the construction of the laws" (*Federalist* 83, 431). Common sense, not precedent, or logic, or reason, but common sense is what judges should use to construct laws—according to Hamilton—and Hamilton gives courts the power to construct laws, something not given to them in a traditional common law setting.[33]

Hamilton moves away from common law thought and closer to Montesquieu and Blackstone, but Hamilton seems to move past Montesquieu and Blackstone in the sense that he is willing to break with the past even more definitively than his two predecessors, and is willing to grant even more authority to the judiciary than either Montesquieu or Blackstone. What separates Hamilton from Montesquieu is less reliance on moderation or history.

The lingering question must be: why does Hamilton grant so much authority to the judiciary? One answer could be that he followed the thought of Montesquieu and Blackstone, was compelled by their reasoning, and took their lessons to the extreme. This answer may be true, but it tells us very little about Hamilton's reasoning. Another answer could be that he saw the judiciary as the best way to promote a national government. I have shown that this too is plausible, but I would also argue that the answer is incomplete. Both of these answers extend from what I consider to be the most accurate approximation for why the judiciary is central to Hamilton's government. Hamilton requires that reason be present, at least somewhat, in order to give direction to the system and to make sure that the passions are properly balancing each other. Reason is the ultimate check on government action, but reason is not present in all those who govern; only the judiciary can be relied upon to harbor reason.[34]

I do not intimate that Hamilton requires a philosopher-king. Like Montesquieu and Blackstone before him, Hamilton makes it clear that liberty and stability can be achieved in the absence of great statesmen so long as the proper institutions are in place. Reason is present within the system itself. The plan which the government is based upon is where reason becomes institutionalized. The system created will pit passion against passion, branch against branch, and faction against faction, which will create a stable environment resulting in a government which will promote the common good. In order to create a system of government that will achieve these ends, reason among the founders is required in order to create a system which embodies reason, a system that will perpetuate the reason of the founders.[35] It is in *Federalist* 49 that we see Hamilton making the point that founding requires reason to sit in judgment (*Federalist* 49, 261–62). However, it is Madison who makes the point most explicit when he says that founding requires "an exemption from the pestilential influence of party animosities" (*Federalist* 10, 47); and I see no reason to believe that Hamilton would disagree with Madison on this point. But while the direct textual evidence is slim, one can put the pieces together in order to show that Hamilton did require the Founders to have reason and interject it into the Constitution. Throughout this section I have shown that Hamilton thinks the efforts in Philadelphia are superior to other founding efforts, as they are writing a constitution deliberately with a broad view of government in mind, and they are informed by the lessons learned from a "new science of politics." However, Hamilton does not expect this sort of knowledge and deliberate action to continue, as that is the whole point of establishing a government with institutional checks on human nature, which he considers to be dominated by passion in most instances. As much as he criticizes human nature for being ruled by passion, he applauds himself and the other Founders for possessing a clear understanding of human nature and how to properly control its ill effects. This means he must attribute reason to himself and the other Founders, since it is reason that has enabled them to create a system which controls passion through a scientific understanding of politics.

Hamilton makes his opinion of the "learned profession" quite obvious, but his reliance on the judiciary to promote reason is not made quite explicit, and must be derived from the duties he gives the judiciary.[36] When Hamilton makes the point that the "learned professions" ought to be the office holders since they "truly form no distinct interest in society . . . they will be the objects of the confidence and choice" (*Federalist* 35, 170), it can be safely assumed that he is referring to lawyers, as they were the most prominent professionals within the state legislatures at the time. Adding strength to the assumption is *Federalist* 78, which praises the virtues of attorneys, while he makes his argument in favor of a strong and independent judiciary. Since the virtues of the learned professions are praised, we can then conclude that these virtues will carry over when these men assume office; however, this is an indefinite conclusion since the passions of men can overtake their reason, especially when they assume office. But, we can logically deduce from what information has already been presented that the judiciary will maintain more reason than the other branches. The path of deduction flows like this: reason is embodied in the Constitution into which the Founders injected their reason while creating the system, the judiciary is supposed to interpret and define the meaning of the Constitution, this process of interpretation makes them the beneficiaries of the Founders' legacy, the legacy of the Founders is reason, which the judiciary would have to inherit in order to interpret the Constitution, each time the judiciary interprets the Constitution it is essentially "re-founding" the Constitution, which makes the judges founders by extension of their interpretative powers. However, the closest thing we get to a direct statement that the judiciary is the reason within government occurs in *Federalist* 49, where Hamilton makes the point that judges embody reason in the government, and the legislature reflects the passions of the people. *Federalist* 49 is concerned with frequent appeals to the people, and if the people are consulted too frequently there might be instability. In fact, when there is disequilibrium in the Constitution, the people cannot be relied on to correct it since it is the people, or attempted appeals to the people, that created the problem. The legislature is the most likely to breach its limits, which would result in disequilibrium since they are the branch which is closest to the people. "The members of the legislative department, on the other hand, are numerous. They are distributed and dwell among the people. Their connections . . . embrace a great proportion of the most influential part of the society" (*Federalist* 49, 263). But it is the judiciary who "are too far removed from the people to share much in their prepossessions" (*Federalist* 49, 263). Both the executive and the legislative might fall victim to temporary popular opinion, which would result in "The passions, therefore, not the reason, of the public, would sit in judgment" (*Federalist* 49, 264). And it is argued in *Federalist* 49 and in *Federalist* 78–83, that the institutional constraints built into the judiciary are too strong to allow this sort of popular infiltration, thus preserving reason in the judiciary.[37] For Hamilton, judges do not always possess reason, but they make reasonable determinations more often than the other branches due to their deliberative nature and removal from popular influences, that is, the institutional design of the judiciary.

It is possible for a nation to establish a stable system which promotes liberty through a favorable turn of history, such as what happened in Montesquieu's England or during the reign of Louis IX, but in order to create such a system intentionally, the founders must possess an understanding of the new science of politics that Hamilton has explicated throughout the *Federalist Papers*. To state more directly, Hamilton argues that prior to the creation of this new science of politics, it was only through random turns of history that a nation could have a government that would promote liberty and stability. But by applying the knowledge that he possesses, a government can be created that promotes liberty and stability through institutional design. While this is certainly consistent with Montesquieu's ambition, Hamilton departs somewhat from Montesquieu by taking another step, moving further away from a reliance on history. According to Hamilton, even history cannot create a system that will be stable; a nation may enjoy stability from time to time, but that nation will eventually fall; it is only through the application of reason that stability will endure. So not only will reason replace history, as it does in Montesquieu and Blackstone, but it is superior to history according to Hamilton. Hamilton's answer to the question of how to establish a stable regime without destroying liberty appears to be certainty, which means the forces of history must be eliminated and replaced with human constructs that are designed to balance the vices of human nature. But, did Hamilton sacrifice liberty for certainty?

NOTES

1. "Tendency" is hardly a word usually associated with an unpredictable process. The point is that history acts at its own pace and through its own means to bring about events which cannot be foreseen by men. To state more simply, man does not know how history will do it, only that it will. Montesquieu understands the tendency and seeks to replicate the tendency through institutional arrangements to make a predictable pace, means, and to make the conclusions foreseeable.

2. The importance of the lessons of history to Montesquieu should be somewhat obvious as he uses historical examples to make his philosophic points, in place of abstract reasoning.

3. According to Judith Shklar (1987), "Linear history was alien to Montesquieu" (Shklar 1987, 50).

4. One purpose of his enterprise was to demonstrate that history can only be understood by drawing out the general causes of things, following the model provided by Thucydides. Through his treatment of history he would be able to understand what was permanently true about politics much in the same way Machiavelli had done.

5. This comes from *Pensees*, but I found it initially in Judith Shklar (1987), page 55.

6. Since there are so many different translations and editions of those translations, using page numbers offers no advantage over simply citing Book and chapter. For references to *The Spirit of the Laws* I will use only book (in Roman numerals) and chapter.

7. Unlike Hamilton, Montesquieu recognizes the positive contributions made by earlier governments.

8. Montesquieu makes very little explicit, as he wants to make the reader work. "But one must not always exhaust a subject that one leaves nothing for the reader to do. It is not a question of making him read but of making him think" (Book XI.20).

9. The threat of Roman law becomes clear after Saint Louis is out of power, and will be discussed below.

10. In the first paragraph of this section I stated that Roman law was the source of deterioration of French/German law. I do not contradict myself when I say that Roman law was one of the reforms that saved French law, as the methods of reform were

different. The Romans used force, whereas Louis used moderate transitions. This is the important distinction; the method used determines what the result will be. This is the point that Montesquieu is making throughout Book XXVIII. However, the Roman law as instituted by Louis did have negative consequences, but the negative consequences occur after Louis leaves power, and new reforms were not correctly instituted to restrict the spread of Roman law.

11. This interpretation of vice is based upon how the passage has been interpreted in a number of different translations.

12. Let this also serve as an example of the dialectical trend of history and how Montesquieu understands that reforms ought to mimic this dialectical trend in history. He praises Louis for following the trend, and this is one reason why Louis is held in such high esteem by Montesquieu. The challenge still remains how to institutionalize the dialectic so a nation does not have to rely on the whim of fortune to bring forward a wise and prudent king.

13. Let us remember that the fall of the Roman Empire was due in part to the Germanic tribes. The visual is unavoidable. The clash between extremes becomes tangible and directly observable in the clash between the Germanic tribes and the Roman Empire. The result of this clash was the rule of Saint Louis, who was able to make a moderate regime by controlling the clash.

14. Thomas Pangle recognizes that "The influential combination of canon and Roman law was generally more reasonable than either the canon law itself or the preexisting system of trial by combat" (Pangle 1973, 287).

15. Perhaps Montesquieu's view of history and the proper balance of power is more influenced by Newton's first law of motion than what is generally recognized.

16. The argument that Montesquieu sees an end of history, or projects the consciousness of men on time in history, is in direct contradiction with Louis Althusser (1977) who reaches a different conclusion in his book *Politics and History*.

17. For Montesquieu, unlike Machiavelli, England was superior to Rome as the English constitution provided greater power for self-correction (*Considerations*, 94).

18. In Montesquieu's view, a moderate regime had previously been merely a byproduct of the randomness of history, and his teaching will allow for a moderate regime to be created without being forced to rely on the forces of history or chance events to create it.

19. He further breaks from the ancients by concluding that law may triumph over all other forces when properly applied, thus eliminating the need for virtue in the rulers, or even morality.

20. The basis for a recent book by Paul Carrese (2003) takes as its thesis that Montesquieu "hides" his treatment of the judiciary, and not only wishes to make the power of the judiciary invisible to the people who are governed by it, but Montesquieu also wishes to "hide" the role of the judiciary to the inattentive reader. And while Carrese does not cite Shklar, she obviously came up with this scenario prior to his writing when she says, "The judicial power is so terrible to mankind that it must be made invisible in some way" (Shklar 1987, 89). But Shklar does not say that Montesquieu hides this point from his readers. If Montesquieu had wished to hide the power of the judiciary from the reader it must have been difficult since his reliance on the

judiciary to balance out the parliament and crown, and to assume the role of the nobility, shows that it cannot be without power as then it would not be able to carry out its given purpose. I do not think it is difficult to come to the conclusion that Montesquieu wants the power of reform to be in the hands of the judiciary. Furthermore, I do not make the claim that Montesquieu "hides" the judiciary—even though I am inclined to that sort of reading for other authors. I only wish to make the point that he writes about the judiciary in the same way he wants it to function, which is in a discreet manner.

21. Montesquieu's heavy reliance on the judiciary to prevent despotism is further evidenced when he says, "In despotic states there is no law; the judge himself is the rule" (VI.5).

22. All references to Blackstone are to *Commentaries on the Laws of England* unless specifically noted otherwise. For the same reason that I used only books and chapters for references to *The Spirit of the Laws*, I will do the same here with the *Commentaries*.

23. "Blackstone, like Coke, defends the common law, but he does so in a way that shows he has absorbed Hobbes's critique. . . . Obviously under the spell of a modern scientific view of nature. . . . For Blackstone, as we have seen, that first principle is self-love; for the earlier thinkers, it was *synderesis*, the faculty of soul that contained the first precepts of actions: seek the good and flee the evil" (Zuckert 2002, 243, 246, 251).

24. History for Blackstone is tradition and custom. Or rather, tradition and custom is the manifestation of history's influence, and precedent is common law's manifestation of tradition and custom.

25. Paul Carrese (2003) makes the strongest argument in favor of the view that Blackstone is seeking to empower the judiciary. I depart from Carrese, and nearly everyone else for that matter, by arguing that Blackstone is a positivist and liberal, and not a common law thinker.

26. Michael Zuckert writes, "His [Blackstone's] treatment of the topic is surely very long compared to the text one can hardly help but think of when one reads this title: the first book of Montesquieu's *Spirit of the Laws*, a work cited approvingly many times in Blackstone's *Commentaries*" (Zuckert 2002, 241).

27. Some of these connections were made by William G. Hammond.

28. All references to *The Federalist Papers* are to the Carey and McClellan edition that has been used throughout.

29. Montesquieu, Blackstone, and Hamilton consider themselves to be more practical than the ancients. They accuse the ancients of promoting virtue over liberty and security, and the three men I have chosen obviously consider virtue to be an unnatural condition for most men.

30. Notice how Hamilton continues to espouse the superiority of the modern regime over the ancient.

31. If Montesquieu had been inclined to make direct statements, this is what he would have said with regard to the judiciary. Hamilton learned the lessons from Montesquieu well as this is the point which Montesquieu makes throughout *The Spirit of the Laws*, but especially in Books XI, XII, and XXVIII.

32. What is also interesting about this passage is that it is the only one in which the judiciary is referred to in *Federalist* 16, which is remarkable considering that it is the medium through which national authority will be manifested. If we recall the earlier sections of Montesquieu and Blackstone, they discussed the judiciary using a similar method.

33. Some commentators argue that *Federalist* 81 offers a more moderate representation of Hamilton's thought on the judiciary than what can be found in *Federalist* 78. However, it should be recognized that *Federalist* 81 does not salvage the common law system, or the system of separation of powers of the much admired Montesquieu. In *Federalist* 81 Hamilton admits that the American system has moved against the British model by taking the final appellate level out of the legislature—the final appellate level in the British common law system was in the House of Lords—and places it in a distinct body of the judiciary which is independent of the legislature. Montesquieu—whom Hamilton openly cites as an authority—admired the British model. In *Federalist* 81 Hamilton moves beyond Montesquieu and abolishes a distinguishing characteristic of the British common law model. When one recognizes this, the teaching of *Federalist* 81 is wholly consistent with, and no less revolutionary than, the reading of Hamilton I have advanced up until this point.

34. It will not surprise the author if there are readers who quarrel with this reading of Hamilton's judiciary. I ask only that if there is a quarrel that it is with my interpretation of the writings I have included, not with those works of Hamilton's which are intentionally omitted. No work can include a discussion of all that has been written by Hamilton. I include those writings that are most representative of his thought.

35. This point was originally made, I believe, by Martin Diamond (1959), though he does not draw the conclusion for the same reason that I do. Diamond seems to say that reason is present because it must be present at the founding. I say that it is present at the founding, according to Hamilton, because it is allowed to be present since the founders have a sound understanding of politics due to their "new science of politics," and have given up trying to mimic historical examples.

36. Hamilton's view of the judiciary seems to be well informed by Montesquieu's observation that "Tribunals of the judiciary must, on the contrary, be coolheaded and, in a way, neutral in all matters of business" (Book VI.6).

37. And while reason may not always be preserved in the judiciary, the passions of the judges are controlled and directed by the institution so that they will result in the proper action. This point is made in an earlier section of this paper concerning how the passions are used.

Conclusion

In the course of creating a new understanding of politics, history, and the judiciary, the three theorists I have presented in chapter 6 eliminated all of the most recognizable hallmarks of the common law system, save one. The preceding chapter has shown that precedent, the separation of law and equity, and the traditional role of the legislature as the sole creator of positive law were purged by Montesquieu, Blackstone, and Hamilton. Instead of being a bulwark against arbitrary government action, the courts were turned into the exact institution that they were intended to protect against under the common law system. The results from chapters 3 to 5 support the claim that the development of the American common law can be more accurately characterized as the dismantling of the common law tradition in America. The argument made throughout chapter 6 is that the dismantling of this system was not by accident, but created by the political philosophy of Alexander Hamilton, whose thoughts find their origin in Montesquieu and Blackstone. For reasons that escape this author, these insights have gone unmentioned by contemporary political scientists. The one explanation that I can provide for why the dismantling of American common law and its implications have been so difficult to uncover has to do with the one hallmark of the common law system which has remained most intact. The jury system was left in place, and remains in place, despite efforts by the legal community and the judiciary to weaken its effectiveness. Since the jury is so visible, efforts to limit its role must be subtle and gradual so as not to raise too much alarm, which makes the efforts undertaken to reform the American jury system consistent with the lessons of Montesquieu and Blackstone.

The jury system was once an institution that protected the rights of the accusers and the accused, and served to represent the community's sense of right and wrong. It was the jury that defined justice in the name of the community. Under the current system, it seems that the jury is in place to serve as a legitimizing force for the judicial process. The jury is perhaps best symbolized as a veil under which judges can hand down decisions without raising much alarm. It was understood by Montesquieu, Blackstone, and Hamilton, and is even understood by contemporary jurists, that to eliminate the jury system would lead to a recognition by serious observers and the general public that there is something awry within the judicial system. Apart from the jury system, all judicial procedures and institutions which were designed to preserve the rule of law and prevent arbitrary action by the government have been either eliminated or so weakened, through redefinition or abandonment, that they are no longer effective restraints. The complexities of something like equity allow for it to be transformed and manipulated without raising much alarm. The jury system, on the other hand, is easily recognizable due to the direct involvement by citizens, which is probably why it has gone through the least dramatic transformation. While the jury system has suffered a similar fate as the other hallmarks of the common law tradition, a façade remains in order to prevent recognition of the transformations taking place. This project warns others not to be fooled into thinking that all is well with the American judiciary simply because we still have the vestiges of a jury system.

The common law system allowed a certain amount of flexibility, and flexibility allows for uncertainty, despite such provisions as precedent, which do preserve a level of consistency. The flexibility of the common law system was what allowed it to act as a bulwark against arbitrary government and potentially authoritarian policies, and flexibility was assured by the presence of a jury. One might say that flexibility is at least one feature that must be in place to help maintain liberty. Flexibility, in the context of the common law tradition, allows for a community to administer justice by allowing the community to determine what laws are applicable and how they ought to be applied. Uncertainty, and by reverse extension so too flexibility, is an undesirable characteristic for Montesquieu, Blackstone, and Hamilton, which is what led them to create systems that would provide predictable outcomes. Somewhere between the unpredictable forces of history and the predictability of human created institutions, those characteristics of the common law system that preserved liberty were lost.

Each time something is added to an equation, the result of the equation changes, and sometimes the result is undesirable. For instance, some of the liberty present in the woods of Germany was compromised when men tried to combine Gothic law with Roman law, and as we have seen, the move toward stability overrode the desire to preserve liberty in France after the reign of Louis IX. So then, would the country have been better off applying Gothic law in an unaltered form? This is perhaps more than just symbolic of what has happened in the American context. Those institutions that Hamilton perceived as weaknesses within the Confederation might have been what allowed for the preservation of liberty, and with the removal of those weaknesses through the creation of a centralized system, the removal of liberty may have also occurred. Through the skillful hand of the three political philosophers presented in chapter 6, the weaknesses of the common law system were eliminated, which would allow the judiciary to be an accomplice in enacting reforms, when before the judiciary was too unreliable due to its unpredictable nature. Was the character of the judiciary as a protector of liberty compromised as a result?

My critique of the reform efforts of Montesquieu, Blackstone, and Hamilton is not intended to be a defense of the judiciary as the only means for protecting liberty. The judiciary is used to illustrate the point that these three men argue that more control is the answer, whereas the common law system assumes that community involvement, respect for the rule of law, and decisions based on a consensus building mechanism is the answer to the question of how best to determine the proper balance between stability and liberty. Perhaps it is true that "As societies become increasingly complex and interdependent, there arises a need for the greater and greater extension of law" (Lence 1995, 161). But law does not have to be, nor does this quote intimate that it must be, determined by an inflexible and centralized system of governance. This project has argued that the theories of our three authors have not only led to a centralized and inflexible system, but that their theories have led to a system in which the rule of law has been compromised by replacing it with the rule of men. It is not law that is the problem; it is how it is created and administered. Doomsday predictions are not a part of this project, nor should they be inferred, as there are still avenues which may be utilized to promote a system which will allow for the community to reassert itself as the rightful determiner of justice and under which the rule of law will prevail. Juries are still present, and may, if citizens take their responsibility as jurors seriously, be used to reclaim the lost traditions of the common law system. This would be a small step in a positive direction. It would help restore a sense of community and responsibility that is essential to a republic's health.

The political implications I have found empirical support for are not the only implications, which is why further research is needed. Future research must look at what effect dismantling the common law system has had on the independence of the judiciary. In one sense the judiciary is more restricted now than it was in the past due to the codification of the law, civil procedure reforms, and sentencing commissions which restrict the discretion of judges. At the same time, the increased power and flexibility that judges gained through the manipulation of the law and equity distinction may counterbalance the restrictiveness of the other reforms. The question of whether judges have more discretion quickly leads to a concern as to whether the discretion they have retained, or gained, has come at the expense of compromising the rule of law. Judicial discretion is essential to the common law, and it is one of the features of the common law that gives it its legitimizing force. But, the common law places its own set of restrictions on judicial discretion in order to preserve the rule of law. There are two related questions that require further investigation: Has the nature of judicial discretion changed as a result of the modifications to the American common law? What effect have these changes had on the rule of law vs. the rule of man?

This study has been an attempt to bring to light many of the changes which have gone unnoticed by political scientists and legal scholars as a result of the dismantling of the common law system in America. Like all first efforts, more questions may have been created than answered. One set of questions has implications for developing democracies. A brief point made at the beginning of this study was that the common law served as a legitimizing force in the early colonies. The common law provided a familiar foundation for the colonists in America and allowed the legislatures to focus on larger issues while allowing the judiciary to fill in the gaps. So what of a nation that is forced to adopt wholesale changes with the only law being a constitution and statutory law? How are the traditions and customs of a people to be respected and integrated into such a system? If the only law is codified law, what happens when an event occurs which is not addressed by the codified law, but is considered an infraction by custom and tradition? Lastly, if the traditions and customs of a people are not given a place in the law or government, what is the legitimizing force which will produce allegiance from the people toward the new set of laws and government? These questions are not restricted to the field of common law, nor are they new questions, as they have been raised by such philosophers as Machiavelli and Montesquieu.

But there is a unique set of questions, which are related to the democratization questions, raised by this study: What debt does the success of American democracy owe to the common law and the judicial branch which is often characterized as being undemocratic? Furthermore, if the United States imposes its model of democracy on other countries without presenting a model of common law first, can the American model be successful? Does the success of a democracy require the presence of an undemocratic institution like a judiciary? Or, is it that the judiciary in a common law system is a democratic institution? These are important questions with relevancy beyond academia that must be answered if democratization is to be more successful than it is currently.

It was my intention to provide a new look at an old system. The common law system has been overlooked for too long. In order to formulate a proper understanding of how this nation was founded, on what philosophical principles the founding was based, and what factors contributed to its success, the role of the common law cannot be ignored. For those interested in the development of American political institutions, federalism, and democratization, the common law needs to be a new point of departure.

Bibliography

Alschuler, Albert W. (2000). *Law Without Values: The Life, Work, and Legacy of Justice Holmes*. Chicago: University of Chicago Press.

Althusser, Louis. (1977) Politics and History: Montesquieu, Rosseau, Hegel, and Marx, 2nd edition. Translated by Ben Brewster. London: NLB

———. (1979). "Pleas Bargaining and Its History." *Columbia Law Review*. Vol. 79.

American Bar Association (1992). *ABA Standards for Criminal Justice, Fair Trial, and Free Press*. Washington, D.C.: American Bar Association.

———. (1984). *Attacking Litigation Costs and Delay: Final Report of the Action Commission to Reduce Court Costs and Delay*. Washington, D.C.: American Bar Association.

———. (1983). *Standards Relating to Juror Use and Management*. Chicago: American Bar Association.

Aristotle (1934). *Nicomachean Ethics*. H. Rackham, trans. Loeb Classical Library. Cambridge, Mass.: Harvard University Press.

———. (1926). *Rhetoric*. J. H. Freese, trans. Loeb Classical Library. Cambridge, Mass.: Harvard University Press.

Ayliffe, John (1734). *A New Product of the Roman Civil Law*. London.

Barrilleaux, Charles, Thomas Holbrook, and Laura Langer (2002). "Electoral Competition, Legislative Balance, and American Welfare Policy." *American Journal of Political Science*. Vol. 46:2.

Bennett, D. Scott, and Allan C. Stam III (1996). "The Duration of Interstate Wars, 1816–1985." *The American Political Science Review*. Vol. 90:2.

Bentham, Jeremy (1977). *A Comment on the Commentaries and A Fragment on Government*. J. H. Burns and H. L. A. Hart, eds. London, England: University of London Anthlone Press.

Berger, Raoul (1939). "Exhaustion of Administrative Remedies." *Yale Law Review*. Vol. 48.

Berry, Frances Stokes, and William D. Berry (1999). "Innovation and Diffusion Models in Policy Research." In *Theories of the Policy Process*, ed. Paul A. Sabatier. Boulder: Westview Press.

——. (1990). "State Lottery Adoptions as Policy: An Event History Analysis." *American Political Science Review*. Vol. 84:2.

Bibby, John F., and Thomas M. Holbrook (2004). "Parties and Elections." In *Politics in The American States: A Comparative Analysis*, 8th Edition. Virginia Gray and Russell L. Hanson, eds. Washington, D.C.: CQ Press.

Bienen, Henry, and Nicolas van de Walle (1992). "A Proportional Hazard Model of Leadership Duration." *Journal of Politics*. Vol. 54:3.

Blackstone, William (1979). *Commentaries on the Laws of England*. Vol. 1–3. Chicago, IL: University of Chicago Press.

——. (1979). *Commentaries on the Laws of England*. 4 Volumes Oxford: Clarendon Press.

——. (1890). *Commentaries on the Laws of England*. 4 Vols. Edited by William G. Hammond. San Francisco, Calif.: Bancroft-Whitney.

——. (1758). *An Analysis of the Laws of England*. 3rd Edition. Oxford.

Bodenheimer, Edgar (1982). "Is Codification an Outmoded Form of Legislation?" *American Journal of Comparative Law*. Vol. 30.

Box-Steffensmeier, Janet M., and Bradford S. Jones (2004). *Event History Modeling: A Guide for Social Scientists*. New York: Cambridge University Press.

Brace, Paul, and Melinda Gann Hall (1995). "Studying Courts Comparatively: The View from the American States." *Political Research Quarterly*. Vol. 48.

——. (1993). "Integrated Models of Judicial Dissent."*Journal of Politics*. Vol. 55.

Brockelbank, J. W. (1954). "The Role of Due Process in American Constitutional Law." *Cornell Law Quarterly*. Vol. 39.

Butler, Jeff E. (1995). "Petty Offenses, Serious Consequences: Multiple Petty Offenses And the Sixth Amendment Right to Jury Trial." *Michigan Law Review* Vol. 94:3.

Butler, Paul (1995). "Racially Based Jury Nullification: Black Power in the Criminal Justice System." *Yale Law Journal*. Vol. 105.

Campbell, Donald T., and Julian C. Stanley (1966). *Experimental and Quasi-Experimental Design for Research*. Chicago: Rand McNally.

Canon, Bradley C., and Lawrence Baum (1981). "Patterns of Adoption of Tort Law Innovations: An Application of Diffusion Theory to Judicial Doctrines." *American Political Science Review*. Vol. 75:1.

Carey, George W., and James McClellan (2001). *The Federalist*. Indianapolis, Ind.: Liberty Fund, Inc.

Carrese, Paul O. (2003). *The Cloaking of Power*. Chicago: University of Chicago Press.

Cicero (1952). *Ad Herennium*. H. Caplan, trans. Loeb Classical Library. Cambridge, Mass.: Harvard University Press.

Clayton, Cornell W., and Gillman, Howard, eds. (1999). *Supreme Court Decision-Making: New Institutionalist Approaches*. Chicago: University of Chicago Press.

Coke, Edward (1974). *The Second Part of the Institutes of the Laws of England: Containing the Exposition of Many Ancient and Other Statutes*. Omni Publications.

———. (1979). *An Abridgement of the Lord Coke's Commentary on Littleton*. Sir Humphrey Davenport, ed. New York: Garland Publishing.

———. *Institutes of the Laws of England.*

Colburn, Trevor, ed. (1962). "Pennsylvania Farmer." *Pennsylvania Magazine of History and Biography*. Vol. 86.

Cook, Charles M. (1981). *The American Codification Movement: A Study of Antebellum Legal Reform*. Westport, Conn.: Greenwood Press.

Corwin, Edward S. (1928). "'The Higher Law' Background of American Constitutional Law." *Harvard Law Review*. Vol. 42.

Curran, D. (1983). "Judicial Discretion and Defendant's Sex." *Criminology*. Vol. 21.

Davis, Kenneth Culp (1958). *Administrative Law Treatise*. St. Paul, Minn.: West Publishing Company.

Diamond, Martin (1959). "Democracy and *The Federalist*: A Reconsideration of the Framers' Intent." *American Political Science Review*. Vol. 53:1.

DiPrima, Stephen R. (1995). "Selecting a Jury in Federal Criminal Trials after Batson and McCollum." *Columbia Law Review*. Vol. 95.

Dorf, Michael C. (1998). "Foreword: The Limits of Socratic Deliberation." *Harvard Law Review*. Vol. 112:4.

Elder, Harold W. (1989). "Trials and Settlements in the Criminal Courts: An Empirical Analysis of Dispositions and Sentencing." *The Journal of Legal Studies*. Vol. 18:1.

Elliot, Jonathan (1941). *The Debates in the Several State Conventions on the Adoption of The Federal Constitution as Recommended by the General Convention at Philadelphia in 1787*. Vol. III. Philadelphia: J. B. Lippincott.

Epstein, Lee and Gary King (2002) "The Rules of Inference." University of Chicago Law Review. Vol. 69:1.

Farrand, Max (1911). *The Records of the Federal Convention of 1787*. 4 Volumes. New Haven, Conn.: Yale University Press.

Fisher, George (2000). "Plea Bargaining's Triumph." *Yale Law Journal*. Vol. 109:5.

Ford, Paul Leicester (1970). *Essays on the Constitution of the United States, Published During its Discussion by the People, 1787–1788*. New York: B. Franklin.

Fortescue, John (1825). *De Laudibus Legum Angliae*. A. Amos, ed. Cambridge, UK: Cambridge University Press.

Frankfurter, Felix, and Thomas G. Corcoran (1926). "Petty Federal Offenses and the Constitutional Guaranty of Trial by Jury." *Harvard Law Review* Vol. 39.

Gerardi, Dino (2000). "Jury Verdicts and Preference Diversity." *American Political Science Review*. Vol. 94.

Gershman, Bennett L. (1986). "Why Prosecutors Misbehave." *Criminal Law Bulletin*. Vol. 22.

Goodenow, John Milton (1819). "Historical Sketches of the Principles and Maxims of American Jurisprudence in Contrast with the Doctrines of the English Common Law on the Subject of Crimes and Punishments." Steubenville, Ohio.

Gray, Virginia (1973). "Innovation in the States: A Diffusion Study." *American Political Science Review*. Vol. 67:2.

Guarnaschelli, Serena, Richard D. McKelvey, and Thomas R. Palfrey (2000). "An Experimental Study of Jury Decision Rules." *American Political Science Review*. Vol. 94.

Hall, Melinda Gann, and Paul Brace (1994). "The Vicissitudes of Death by Decree: Forces Influencing Capital Punishment in State Supreme Courts." *Social Science Quarterly*. Vol. 75.

Hallifax, Samuel (1775). *An Analysis of the Roman Civil Law*. Cambridge, UK: Cambridge University Press.

Hammons, Christopher W. (1999). "Was James Madison Wrong? Rethinking the American Preference for Short, Framework-Oriented Constitutions." *The American Political Science Review*. Vol. 93:4.

Hartmus, Diane M., and James P. Levine (1998). "Videotaped Trial Transcripts for Juror Deliberations." *Judicature*. Vol. 82.

Hemmens, Craig, Kristin Strom, and Elicia Schlegel (1998). "Gender Bias in the Courts: A Review of the Literature." *Sociological Imagination*. Vol. 35.

Hogue, Arthur R. (1986). Reprint. *Origins of the Common Law*. Indianapolis, Ind.: Liberty Fund, Inc.

Holmes, Malcolm D., Howard C. Daudistel, and William A. Taggart (1992). "Plea Bargaining Policy and State District Court Caseloads: An Interrupted Time Series Analysis." *Law & Society Review*. Vol. 26:1.

Horwitz, Morton J. (1977). *The Transformation of American Law: 1780–1860*. Cambridge, Mass.: Harvard University Press.

Ingersoll, Henry H. (1911). "Confusion of Law and Equity." *Yale Law Journal*. Vol. 21.

Judson, Frederick N. (1910). "A Modern View of the Law Reforms of Jeremy Bentham." *Columbia Law Review*. Vol. 10:1.

Kadish, Sanford H. (1978). "Codifiers of the Criminal Law: Wechsler's Predecessors." *Columbia Law Review*. Vol. 78.

Kames, Lord Henry Home, (1972). *Elements of Criticism*. Vol. 1. New York: Garland Publishing.

Kent, James (1836). *Commentaries on American Law*, 3rd Edition. New York.

Ketcham, Ralph, ed. (1986). *The Anti-Federalist Papers and the Constitutional Convention Debates: The Clashes and The Compromises That Gave Birth to Our Form Of Government*. New York: Signet Classic.

King, Gary (1986). "How Not to Lie with Statistics: Avoiding Common Mistakes in Quantitative Political Science." *American Journal of Political Science*. Vol. 30:3.

King, Gary, Robert O. Keohane, and Sidney Verba (1994). *Designing Social Inquiry: The Scientific Inference in Qualitative Research*. Princeton, N.J.: Princeton University Press.

King, Nancy J. (1993). "Postconviction Review of Jury Discrimination: Measuring the Effects of Jurors Race on Jury Decisions." *Michigan Law Review*. Vol. 92.

Landsman, Stephan (1999). "The Civil Jury in America." *Law and Contemporary Problems*. Vol. 62.

Langbein, John H. (1992). "On the Myth of Written Constitutions: The Disappearance of Criminal Jury Trial." *Harvard Journal of Law and Public Policy*. Vol. 15.

———. (1979). "Understanding the Short History of Plea Bargaining." *Law and Society Review*. Vol. 13.

Langer, Laura (2002). *Judicial Review in State Supreme Courts: A Comparative Study*. Albany, N.Y.: State University of New York Press.

Lanni, Adriaan (1999). "Jury Sentencing in Noncapital Cases: An Idea Whose Time Has Come (Again)?" *Yale Law Journal*. Vol. 108.

Laycock, Douglas (2002). *Modern American Remedies: Cases and Materials 3rd Edition*. New York: Aspen Publishers, Inc.

———. (1993). "The Triumph of Equity." *Law and Contemporary Problems*. Vol. 56.

———. (1991). *The Death of the Irreparable Injury Rule*. Oxford, UK: Oxford University Press.

———. (1990). "The Death of the Irreparable Injury Rule." *Harvard Law Review*. Vol. 103.

Lear, Elizabeth T. (1993). "Is Conviction Irrelevant?" *UCLA Law Review*. Vol. 40.

Lence, Ross M. (1995). "Is Civic Order Possible in the Modern City?" In *This Will Hurt: The Restoration of Virtue and Civic Order*. Digby Anderson, ed. The Social Affairs Unit, A National Review Book.

Lettow, Rennee B. (1994). "Reviving Grand Jury Presentments." *Yale Law Journal*. Vol. 103.

Levine, James P. (1996). "The Impact of Sequestration on Juries." *Judicature*. Vol. 79.

Llewellyn, Karl (1931). "Some Realism about Realism—Responding to Dean Pound." *Harvard Law Review*.

Lobban, Michael (1987). "Blackstone and the Science of Law." *The Historical Journal*. Vol. 30:2.

Lodge, Henry Cabot, ed. (1885–1886). *The Works of Alexander Hamilton*. New York: G. P. Putnam's Sons.

Manning, John F. (2001). "Textualism and the Equity of the Statute." *Columbia Law Review*. Vol. 101.

McCaffery, Edward J., Daniel J. Kahneman, and Matthew L. Spitzer (1995). "Framing the Jury: Cognitive Perscriptives on Pain and Suffering Awards." *Virginia Law Review*. Vol. 81.

McCloskey, Robert G. (1967). *The Works of James Wilson*. 2 Volumes. Cambridge, Mass.: Harvard University Press.

McDonald, Forrest (1985). *Norvus Ordo Seclorum: The Intellectual Origins of the Constitution*. Lawrence: University Press of Kansas.

McDowell, Gary L. (1993). "Coke, Corwin and the Constitution: The 'Higher Law Background' Reconsidered." *Review of Politics*. Vol. 63:2.

———. (1982). *Equity and the Constitution*. Chicago: University of Chicago Press.

Mintrom, Michael (2000). *Policy Entrepreneurs and School Choice*. Washington, D.C.: Georgetown University Press.

———. (1997). "Policy Entrepreneurs and the Diffusion of Innovation." *The American Journal of Political Science*. 41:1.

Mintrom, Michael, and Sandra Vergari (1998). "Policy Networks and Innovation Diffusion: The Case of State Education Reforms." *Journal of Politics*. Vol. 60:1.

Montesquieu (2002). *The Spirit of the Laws*. Anne M. Cohler, Basia C. Miller, and Harold S. Stone, trabs, and ed. Cambridge: Cambridge University Press.

——. (1999). "The Temporal Diffusion of Morality Policy: The Case of Death Penalty Legislation in the American States." *Policy Studies Journal*. Vol. 27:1.

——. (1968). *Considerations on the Causes of the Greatness of the Romans and Their Decline*. David Lowenthal, trans. Allan Bloom, ed. Ithaca, NY: Cornell University Press.

——. (1949). *The Spirit of the Laws*. Thomas Nugent, trans. F. Neumann, ed. New York.

Mooney, Christopher Z., and Mei-Hsien Lee (1995). "Legislative Morality in the American States: The Case of Pre-Roe Abortion Regulation Reform." *American Journal of Political Science*. Vol. 39:1.

Morris, Richard B. (1957). *Alexander Hamilton and the Founding of the Nation*. New York.

Nelson, William E. (1994). *Americanization of the Common Law: The Impact of Legal Change on Massachusetts Society, 1760–1830*. Atlanta: University of Georgia Press.

Pangle, Thomas L. (1973). *Montesquieu's Philosophy of Liberalism: A Commentary on The Spirit of the Laws*. Chicago: University of Chicago Press.

Peltason, J. W. (1961). *Fifty-Eight Lonely Men: Southern Federal Judges and School Desegregation*. New York: Harcourt, Brace, and World.

Ranney, Austin (1976). "Parties in State Politics." In *Parties in the American States: A Comparative Analysis*, 3rd Edition. Herbert Jacob and Kenneth Vines, eds. Boston: Little Brown.

Rosen, Mark D. (1994). "What Has Happened to the Common Law?—Recent American Codifications, and their Impact on Judicial Practice and the Law's Subsequent Development." *Wisconsin Law Review*.

Rosenberg, Gerald N. (1991). *The Hollow Hope: Can Courts Bring About Social Change?* Chicago: University of Chicago Press.

Rosenthal, Albert J. (1978). "Discord and Dissatisfaction: Section 1–207 of the Uniform Commercial Code." *Columbia Law Review*. Vol. 78.

Rubinstein, Michael L., and Teresa J. White (1979). "Alaska's Ban on Plea Bargaining." *Law & Society Review*. Vol. 13:2.

Saint Germain, Christopher (1974). *Doctor and Student*. T. Plucknett and J. Barton, eds.

Sauer, Kristen K. (1995). "Informed Conviction: Instructing the Jury about Mandatory Sentencing Consequences." *Columbia Law Review*. Vol. 95.

Schafran, L. H. (1990). "Overwhelming Evidence: Reports on Gender Bias in the Courts." *Trial*. Vol. 26.

Schattschneider, E. E. (1960). *The Semisovereign People: A Realist's View of Democracy In America*. New York: Holt, Rinehart, and Winston.

Schubert, Glendon A. (1964). *Judicial Decision Making*. New York: Free Press of Glencoe.

Schulhofer, Stephen J. (1984). "Is Plea Bargaining Inevitable?" *Harvard Law Review*. Vol. 97:5.

Segal, Jeffery A., and Harold J. Spaeth (2002). *The Supreme Court and the Attitudinal Model Revisited*. New York: Cambridge University Press.

Shklar, Judith N. (1987). *Montesquieu*. New York: Oxford University Press.

———. (1977). "Publius and the Science of the Past." *Yale Law Journal*. Vol. 86:6.

Siegan, Bernard (2001). *Property Rights: From Magna Carta to the Fourteenth Amendment*. New Brunswick, N.J.: Transaction Publishers.

Smith, Douglas A. (1986). "The Plea Bargaining Controversy." *The Journal of Criminal Law and Criminology*. Vol. 77:3.

Steele, Walter W., and Elizabeth G. Thornburg (1991). "Jury Instructions: A Persistent Failure to Communicate." *Judicature*. Vol. 74.

Stoner, James R. (2003). *Common-Law Liberty: Rethinking American Constitutionalism*. Lawrence: University Press of Kansas.

———. (1992). *Common Law and Liberal Theory: Coke, Hobbes, and the Origins of American Constitutionalism*. Lawrence: University Press of Kansas.

Storing, Herbert J. (1981a). *The Complete Anti-Federalist*. Vol. II and IV–VI. Chicago: University of Chicago Press.

———. (1981b). *What the Anti-Federalists were for*. Chicago: The University of Chicago Press.

Story, Joseph (1829–1833). "Law, Legislation, and Codes." In *Encyclopedia Americana*, Vol. 7. Philadelphia.

Surbin, Stephen N. (1987). "How Equity Conquered Common Law: The Federal Rules of Civil Procedure in Historical Perspective." *University of Pennsylvania Law Review*. Vol. 135.

Taft, William H. (1969). *Taft Papers, 1890–1930*. Washington, D.C.: Library of Congress.

Tansill, Charles Callan, ed. (1972). "Declaration and Resolves of the First Continental Congress, October 14, 1774." Reprinted in *Making of the American Republic: The Great Documents 1774–1789*. New Rochelle, N.Y.: Arlington House.

Tarr, G. Alan (1977). *Judicial Impact and State Supreme Courts*. Lexington, Mass.: Lexington Books.

Tocqueville, Alexis de (2000). *Democracy in America*. Harvey C. Mansfield and Delba A., trans. and ed. Winthrop. Chicago: University of Chicago Press.

Walker, Jack L. (1969). "The Diffusion of Innovations among the American States." *American Political Science Review*. Vol. 63:2.

Warren, Charles (1911). *A History of the American Bar*. Boston: Little Brown.

Weiher, Gregory R. and Jon Lorence (1991). "Growth in State Government Employment: A Time Series Analysis." *Western Political Quarterly* Vol. 44:2.

Welch, Susan, and Kay Thompson (1980). "The Impact of Federal Incentives on State Policy Innovation." *American Journal of Political Science*. Vol. 24:3.

Whitman, James Q. (1991). "Why Did the Revolutionary Lawyers Confuse Custom and Reason?" *University of Chicago Law Review*. Vol. 58:4.

Wikler, N. J. (1980). "On the Judicial Agenda for the 80s: Equal Treatment for Men and Women in the Courts." *Judicature*. Vol. 64.

Wilson, James. (1967) The Works of James Wilson. Vol. 1. Edited by Robert Green McCloskey. Cambridge, MA: Harvard University Press

Zuckert, Michael P. (2002). *Launching Liberalism: On Lockean Political Philosophy*. Lawrence: University Press of Kansas.

Index